The Constitution of One: How the Bill of Rights Protects the Sovereign Man & Woman

Sovereign Foundations: Liberty, Rights, Consent, Volume 1

Roger Davies

Published by TWON Publications, 2025.

THE CONSTITUTION OF ONE: HOW THE BILL OF RIGHTS PROTECTS THE SOVEREIGN MAN & WOMAN

First edition. September 9, 2025.

ISBN: 979-8232912338

Written by Roger Davies.

Table of Contents

Introduction 1
Chapter 1: The Source of Rights 6
Chapter 2: The First Amendment – Voice of the Sovereign 12
Chapter 3: The Second Amendment – The Right to Defend 18
Chapter 4: The Third Amendment – Home as Castle 24
Chapter 5: The Fourth Amendment – The Right to Be Left Alone 29
Chapter 6: The Fifth Amendment – No Man Bound Without Consent 34
Chapter 7: The Sixth Amendment – The Jury as Shield 39
Chapter 8: The Seventh Amendment – Commerce and Common Law . 44
Chapter 9: The Eighth Amendment – Limits on Punishment 49
Chapter 10: The Ninth Amendment – Rights Beyond Writing 54
Chapter 11: The Tenth Amendment – The Power of the People 58
Chapter 12: The Constitution of One – Living Sovereignty 62
Conclusion 66

This book is dedicated to every man and woman in America who remembers that freedom comes from birth, not from government.

To those who hold fast to the Bill of Rights, as evidence of their sovereignty, who speak truth when silence is demanded, and who stand firm when authority overreaches.

Your resolve ensures that liberty is not forgotten but lived and passed forward as the living constitution of one

Introduction

Freedom is not granted by paper. It is not written into existence by a congress or a court. It is not bestowed by officials or rulers. Freedom is the condition of life itself. You are born with it. No one can take it from you without your consent.

Yet from the moment you draw breath, the system moves to persuade you that freedom is not yours. It presents papers, rules, and offices as though they were the source of authority. It trains you to obey, to apply for permission, and to submit to titles that were never yours. The trick is subtle. You are led to believe that your rights exist because a document says so, rather than because you exist.

The Constitution of the United States, and especially the Bill of Rights, is often taught as the foundation of American freedom. Schools present it as the moment when liberty began. Politicians praise it as the source of authority. Judges quote it as if it were the fountain of justice. But the truth is different. The Constitution did not create freedom. The Bill of Rights did not grant rights. These documents only recorded what already existed.

The men who signed the Constitution were not inventing liberty. They were acknowledging it. They knew that life itself was the source of rights. The Bill of Rights was evidence, not creation. It was written proof that certain truths were beyond government.

For the sovereign man or woman today, this is the key. You do not look to paper for your freedom. You look to yourself. You are the Constitution of one. The Bill of Rights does not hand you rights. It reminds you that those rights cannot be taken.

Officials twist this truth. They say government grants rights. They say freedom is limited to what is written. They say statutes outrank birthrights. This is deception. The Ninth Amendment itself admits that not all rights are written. It says that the rights of the people are not denied simply because they are not listed. That statement alone proves that freedom comes first, and paper comes second.

Think about speech. The First Amendment did not create the right to speak. People spoke long before 1791. The amendment only acknowledged that government had no authority to silence the voice of the people. The same is true of every amendment. The right to defend yourself, the right to property, the right to be secure in your home, the right to trial by jury, the right to limit punishment, the right to powers not delegated, all of these existed first. The amendments are witnesses, not creators.

This distinction matters because it changes where you stand. If you believe rights come from government, then you must ask permission. If you believe rights come from life, then you stand as sovereign. The government can write papers, but it cannot take away what it never gave.

The Constitution of one means you carry freedom within you. You are not waiting for congress to recognize it.

You are not waiting for courts to confirm it. You are not waiting for officials to approve it.

You know that the Bill of Rights is evidence, not authority. It is proof that the living man or woman outranks any office or statute.

The danger of forgetting this is clear. When people believe government grants rights, they surrender sovereignty. They beg for privileges. They accept licenses as if they were necessary. They obey policies as if they were law. They become subjects instead of sovereigns. That is not freedom. That is servitude dressed in patriotic colors.

Look around. You will see people defending statutes that limit their own freedom. You will hear them say that free speech does not include certain words. You will hear them say that the right to bear arms depends on permission slips. You will hear them say that privacy depends on paperwork. These beliefs come from forgetting that freedom is first. They come from confusing evidence with source.

This book is written to set the record straight. It is not about politics. It is not about parties or platforms. It is about principle. The Bill of Rights belongs to you because it only mirrors what you already are. Each amendment will be examined not as a grant from government but as a recognition of your standing as a sovereign man or woman.

You will see how the First Amendment proves that your voice is free. You will see how the Second proves that you may defend yourself.

You will see how the Fourth proves that your home is your castle. You will see how the Fifth proves that no man can be bound without consent.

You will see how the Sixth and Seventh prove that true justice belongs to juries of peers, not corporate courts. You will see how the Eighth proves that punishment cannot be used as tyranny. You will see how the Ninth proves that your rights extend beyond the page. You will see how the Tenth proves that power rests with the people, not with distant rulers.

This is the Constitution of one. It is the truth that the living man or woman is the highest authority in their own life. It is the reminder that paper only confirms what you already are. It is the shield against statutes, policies, and officials who pretend to be masters.

The danger of forgetting that freedom comes first is not theory. History shows what happens when men and women trust governments to grant rights. Every tyranny begins with promises of safety and order. Every regime that enslaves first convinces the people that their rights are gifts from the state. Once people accept that story, the state can claim the power to take those gifts away.

That is why the Bill of Rights was written in clear language. The First Amendment says "Congress shall make no law." The Second says "the right of the people shall not be infringed." The Fourth says "shall not be violated." Again and again the words are negative, binding government, not the people. The purpose was not to give rights but to restrain rulers.

Yet officials today act as though those restraints do not exist. They pass statutes and claim they override amendments. They expand agencies and pretend they outrank natural law. They build courts that operate as corporations and insist those courts are the final authority. None of this is lawful. It is only assumption. It survives only because people consent, remain silent, or forget their standing.

The Constitution of one is the reminder that you do not need to wait for officials to honor the Bill of Rights. You can honor it yourself by living in truth. You can stand as a sovereign man or woman, knowing that each amendment is your evidence, not your permission slip. You are not asking. You are affirming.

Think about the power of the jury. The Sixth and Seventh Amendments confirm trial by jury as a shield for the people. A jury is not meant to be a tool of the judge. It is meant to be the voice of the community, the peers of the accused. When a jury refuses to convict under an unjust statute, it proves that the people outrank government codes. That is nullification.

It is the living proof that the Constitution of one extends into the Constitution of the many. Yet most jurors are never told this. They are instructed to obey the judge. They are told they have no power. That is a lie.

The same deception applies to the Second Amendment. The right to bear arms did not begin in 1791. It began the moment the first man or woman picked up a tool to defend life. The amendment only acknowledged what was already there.

Yet politicians today speak as if the right exists only with their permission. They pass statutes limiting arms and insist those statutes have authority. But the truth remains: government cannot take what it never gave.

The Ninth Amendment is the most revealing. It says that the listing of rights in the Constitution shall not be used to deny other rights retained by the people. This single line destroys the claim that rights come only from paper. It admits openly that many rights are not written down. They belong to you simply because you are alive. Privacy, travel, contract, family, property, all of these flow from life itself. The Ninth Amendment is proof that the Constitution itself acknowledges its own limits.

The Tenth Amendment makes the same point about power. It says that powers not delegated to the federal government are reserved to the states or the people. Federal officials ignore this daily. They act as if Washington holds unlimited authority. But the text itself says otherwise. Powers not granted remain with the people. That means with you. A single man or woman has the same standing as a state. The union is a compact of equals. The individual is not property of the collective.

This book will not tell you that freedom is easy. It is not. To stand in sovereignty means facing resistance. You will be mocked by neighbors. You will be questioned by family. You will be threatened by officials. But the remedy is not anger or rebellion.

It is honor. To stand in honor is to speak calmly, to ask for proof, and to refuse false obligations. The Bill of Rights supports you. It stands as evidence that the living man or woman outranks any statute.

The Constitution of one is not rebellion. It is responsibility. It does not excuse harm or fraud. It does not mean chaos. It means living by natural law: do no harm, cause no loss, commit no fraud. When you live by these principles, you live above statutes. You prove that freedom is not lawlessness. It is order grounded in truth.

Paper cannot save you if you forget who you are. Courts will twist words. Politicians will ignore text. Officials will threaten. But none of them can erase the fact that you are alive, sovereign, and free. The Bill of Rights is valuable not because it creates your freedom, but because it records it. It is the evidence you can point to when officials pretend otherwise.

Every chapter of this book will take one amendment and place it back in your hands. You will see the First as your living voice. You will see the Second as your shield.

You will see the Third as proof that your home is your castle. You will see the Fourth as your right to be left alone. You will see the Fifth as your guard against forced contracts. You will see the Sixth and Seventh as your right to judgment by peers, not officials. You will see the Eighth as your defense against punishment as control. You will see the Ninth as the open door to rights not listed. You will see the Tenth as the foundation of power resting with the people.

When you finish this journey, you will not think of the Constitution as a dusty document in a museum. You will see it as a mirror. You will see yourself in it. You will remember that you are the Constitution of one. The Bill of Rights is the testimony. You are the source.

This is the path of sovereignty. It begins with knowledge. It grows with honor. It is lived through daily choices. The Constitution of one is not a theory. It is a way of life.

Chapter 1: The Source of Rights

Every man and woman alive today carries within them rights that no paper created and no office can take away. These rights are not permissions. They are not privileges. They are not favors granted by a ruler. They are woven into life itself. They flow from the simple fact that you are alive.

The mistake of modern society is to believe that rights are written into existence. People are taught that freedom came from the Constitution, that justice was created by Congress, and that protection flows from courts. This belief is dangerous because it shifts authority away from the living and into the hands of officials. It turns rights into privileges that can be revoked. It reduces sovereignty to paperwork.

Look at history before the Constitution. Long before 1787, men and women lived in communities guided by conscience, custom, and natural law. They knew instinctively that harm was wrong, theft was wrong, fraud was wrong. No government had to teach these truths. They were self-evident. Every tribe, every settlement, every family recognized them. These principles existed across cultures and continents.

The founders of America did not invent rights. They recognized them. They spoke of them as unalienable. That word matters. It means rights cannot be sold, transferred, or surrendered. They belong to you as part of life. You do not receive them from outside. You hold them within.

The Constitution and Bill of Rights are often praised as if they created freedom. In truth, they only confirmed it. They are testimony, not source. They were written to restrain government, not to define the people. When the First Amendment says that Congress shall make no law abridging speech, it is not giving you a right. It is admitting that government has no power to silence you. When the Second Amendment says the right to bear arms shall not be infringed, it is not handing you that right. It is acknowledging that you already held it.

This distinction changes everything. If rights come from government, then government can take them away. If rights come from life, then government cannot touch them without your consent. That is why rulers prefer to teach that rights are granted. It places them in the position of master. It persuades people to beg for favors. It makes freedom a license instead of a birthright.

Think about how this plays out in daily life. People apply for licenses to marry, to drive, to build, to trade. They believe they must seek permission for acts that are already lawful. They confuse rights with privileges. A license is not freedom. It is the opposite. It is a contract that admits you have no right unless you pay tribute and obey conditions. The living man or woman never needed that permission. The right existed already.

The maxim of law is clear: what is self-evident does not require proof. Life itself is proof of rights. Breath is proof.

Thought is proof. Speech is proof. No official seal adds to this. No stamp of approval creates it. The role of paper is only to record what is.

The Bill of Rights was written as a reminder. It was not written for you. It was written for government. It says to Congress, to courts, to presidents, to every office: these things you cannot do. It binds them, not you. That is why each amendment speaks in terms of restriction. "Shall not be infringed." "Shall not be violated." "No person shall." The language is negative because the purpose is to chain authority, not to chain life.

When you remember this, fear begins to fade. You stop looking to officials as masters. You stop waiting for permission. You see that you are the Constitution of one. You are the source of your own freedom. Paper only confirms it.

This does not mean you act in chaos. Natural law remains the standard. Do no harm. Cause no loss. Commit no fraud. Keep the peace. These principles are eternal. They require no legislature. They require only conscience. A free man or woman lives within them by choice, not by coercion. That is the difference between sovereignty and servitude.

The modern system works by reversing this order. It tells you that rights come from statutes. It tells you that obligations exist before consent. It tells you that silence is not agreement, but duty. These are lies repeated until they are believed. But belief does not make truth. The truth is that statutes are contracts. They apply only with consent. Rights do not depend on contracts. They exist by birth.

Ask yourself simple questions. Did you sign a contract surrendering your right to speak? Did you agree to be searched without cause? Did you consent to taxation as tribute at birth? The answer is no. No such contracts exist. The presumption of government authority rests on silence, not agreement. And silence is dishonor.

The Bill of Rights is valuable because it gives you evidence when officials demand obedience. You can point to it and say, here is proof that even your own system admits these rights exist. But the stronger truth is that you do not need the paper to prove it. You are the living man or woman. You are the source. The Constitution only mirrors what you already are.

This is why rulers work so hard to bury natural law. Schools do not teach it. Courts do not apply it. Media ridicules it. They know that once people remember the source of rights, the entire structure of control collapses. A sovereign who knows the truth cannot be ruled without consent.

To see the source of rights clearly, look at the language of the Declaration of Independence. It declared that all men are created equal, that they are endowed by their Creator with certain unalienable Rights, and that governments are instituted to secure those rights. Notice the order. The Creator gives rights. Government is formed afterward. Its only role is to secure, not to grant. If government fails in that duty, it loses legitimacy. This principle is central to the American spirit, yet it is ignored by those who seek control.

Officials prefer to reverse the order. They speak as if the Constitution created rights and as if government is the master of liberty. Schools repeat this message until children accept it without thought. By adulthood most people believe that without government there is no order, no protection, no freedom. This belief is false. History shows the opposite. Communities lived with order long before bureaucracies. Families and tribes honored life long before legislatures. True law existed before government offices were built.

The Constitution of one begins with this truth. Your rights do not begin with paper. They do not depend on votes or rulings. They exist because you exist. That is why they are unalienable. No act of Congress, no court opinion, and no presidential order can erase them. The only way they appear lost is through your own consent or silence.

Consider speech again. The First Amendment records that Congress shall make no law abridging freedom of speech. Yet every day people are silenced through policy, regulation, or threat. Officials tell you that you cannot speak freely on certain platforms, in certain places, or on certain topics. They pretend that your voice depends on their permission. But no man gave you breath, and no man can take it. Speech is an act of life, not of law. The amendment is only evidence. The true source is you.

Consider self-defense. The Second Amendment affirms that the right to keep and bear arms shall not be infringed. Many argue about its wording, about militias and regulation. But look deeper.

Did life itself not give you the right to defend yourself and your family? Would you be alive if your ancestors had no tools to defend themselves against predators, invaders, or tyrants? The amendment did not grant the right. It acknowledged the obvious. Defense is part of survival. Government cannot erase what nature itself established.

Consider property. The Fifth Amendment affirms that no person shall be deprived of property without due process of law, nor shall private property be taken for public use without just compensation. Again, property rights did not begin in 1791. They existed whenever a man or woman worked, built, or created. The right to the fruit of your labor is inseparable from life. No paper adds to it. The amendment only serves as a barrier against government theft. The source is labor and life, not statute.

The same pattern runs through every right. Privacy, trial by jury, protection against cruel punishments, limits on federal power, all of these were already part of natural law. The Bill of Rights is testimony, not creation. It is evidence placed on record to restrain rulers. When you grasp this, you stop treating paper as master. You recognize yourself as sovereign.

The maxim "consent makes the law" explains why rulers deny the true source of rights. If people knew they were the source, they would stop consenting to false obligations. They would question every demand. They would withhold consent until proof was shown.

The system cannot survive in that environment. That is why it depends on ignorance. That is why courts and schools rarely discuss natural law. That is why ridicule is directed at anyone who speaks of sovereignty.

But knowledge restores balance. Once you remember that rights come from life, fear weakens. You no longer tremble when officials wave papers. You no longer rush to sign forms. You no longer assume that silence protects you. You stand and speak. You ask for proof. You demand contract. You act in honor. By doing so you remind the system that it has no authority without you.

This is not rebellion. It is restoration. It is not defiance. It is truth. To stand in the source of rights is to live in alignment with natural law. You respect others, you honor agreements, you cause no harm. You take full responsibility for your choices. Sovereignty is not license to injure. It is duty to live in truth. The system paints sovereignty as chaos because it fears responsibility in the hands of the people. In reality, a sovereign man or woman is more orderly than any bureaucrat because their word is bond and their honor is intact.

History is filled with proof. Jury nullification, where jurors refuse to convict under unjust laws, is one example. Communities that lived by common law before the rise of statutes are another. Even the founders themselves acted as sovereigns when they declared independence. They did not beg for permission. They did not wait for approval.

They stood in the source of rights and declared government subordinate to life. That spirit lives on in every man and woman willing to remember.

The challenge is to act daily from that source. Each time you sign without reading, you surrender sovereignty. Each time you pay without questioning, you accept a contract. Each time you answer to a name in capital letters without thought, you step into fiction. These habits keep you bound. To break them requires awareness. You pause. You ask. You rebut. You stand as the living. You remember the source.

The Constitution of one is the path back to memory. It is the reminder that you are not property. You are not a subject. You are not a debtor by birth. You are sovereign. You are the source of your rights. The Bill of Rights is evidence for you to use when officials pretend otherwise, but the deeper proof is your own existence.

This chapter began by asking where rights come from. The answer is simple. They come from life. They come from the Creator. They come from breath, conscience, and honor. Government cannot add to them. Government cannot subtract from them. Government can only recognize them or attempt to conceal them. Your task as a sovereign is to live in recognition, not concealment.

In the chapters ahead, we will look at each amendment and see how it confirms what you already know.

We will see how the First affirms voice, the Second affirms defense, the Fourth affirms privacy, the Fifth affirms property, and so on. Each one is a mirror, not a source. Each one testifies that you are the Constitution of one.

When you know the source of rights, fear disappears. Officials cannot frighten you with papers. Judges cannot bind you with words on a page. Politicians cannot reduce you to a subject. You are living proof that freedom does not come from government. It comes from within.

Chapter 2: The First Amendment – Voice of the Sovereign

The first act of sovereignty is speech. To speak is to declare that you exist. It is to give voice to thought, to conscience, and to truth. No government created this ability. No statute sustains it. The power to speak is inseparable from life itself. That is why the First Amendment is placed first. It is the cornerstone of liberty because without it no other right can be defended.

The text is clear: "Congress shall make no law respecting an establishment of religion, or prohibiting the free exercise thereof; or abridging the freedom of speech, or of the press; or the right of the people peaceably to assemble, and to petition the Government for a redress of grievances." These words are not a gift. They are a restraint. They do not hand you a right. They bind Congress from touching what was never theirs to control.

The sovereign man or woman knows that voice is sacred. Speech is not limited to words on a page or sounds in the air. It is the expression of will. It includes faith, assembly, and petition. It is the act of standing in truth before the world. Without this act, sovereignty is silent and therefore invisible. With it, sovereignty is alive and undeniable.

Look at the pattern of history. Tyrants always begin by silencing speech. They censor, punish, or intimidate those who speak truth. They close assemblies, burn books, and punish dissenters.

They fear words because words reveal deception. A lie cannot survive when truth is spoken openly. That is why rulers seek control of speech. But that control is never lawful. It is only force dressed in authority.

The First Amendment affirms that government has no such power. Yet officials still attempt to limit speech through statutes, regulations, and policies. They create zones where speech is "permitted." They pass laws against certain words or symbols. They censor in the name of safety, order, or harmony. All of these actions are unlawful because they assume government is the source of rights. The truth is the opposite. Government cannot abridge what it never gave.

Freedom of speech is linked directly to freedom of conscience. The amendment protects religion because faith is an expression of conscience. No man can dictate another's conscience. It belongs to the individual. To compel belief or practice is to enslave the soul. That is why the amendment bars government from establishing religion or prohibiting its free exercise. Once again, the principle is recognition, not creation.

Consider assembly. The right of the people to gather peaceably is not a privilege. It is the natural result of community. Men and women gather to share, to decide, to act. No permission slip was ever required for families or tribes to meet. The amendment acknowledges that government cannot forbid it.

Yet today permits are demanded for rallies, marches, and even small gatherings. Officials act as if they can approve or deny. This is fraud. The right to assemble existed long before permits.

Petition is the final part of the amendment. To petition is to demand accountability from rulers. It is the voice of the people directed at those who claim authority. Petition is not begging. It is not a request for favors. It is the lawful right to require answers. It is the act of placing grievances on record so that rulers cannot pretend ignorance. When government ignores petitions, it stands in dishonor.

The sovereign perspective sees all of this as one principle: the right to express life without interference. Speech, faith, assembly, and petition are all expressions of the living man or woman. They cannot be separated. They cannot be reduced to paperwork. They cannot be licensed. They exist by birth.

Why then do so many accept restrictions on speech? The answer is fear and habit. Schools train children to ask permission before speaking. Media conditions adults to silence themselves when their words are unpopular. Courts punish those who challenge authority in plain language. Over time people learn to censor themselves. They forget that the First Amendment does not grant freedom of speech. It removes government from the conversation.

From the standpoint of law, silence is dangerous. He who fails to deny agrees. If you remain silent when false authority claims power, you appear to consent. Speech is therefore not only a right but a duty. You speak to rebut presumption. You place truth on the record. You ask questions that expose fraud. Each word spoken in honor is a shield. Each affidavit written in truth is a sword. Speech is the remedy against silence.

The power of the First Amendment becomes clear when you remember its place in natural law. Speech is not just protected by paper. It is protected by conscience. A lie cannot erase truth once spoken. A government cannot erase conscience once declared. That is why sovereign men and women speak even when threatened. Their voice carries authority greater than statutes.

Think of the many who stood before power and spoke truth. From the early colonists protesting British taxes, to abolitionists demanding freedom for the enslaved, to jurors refusing unjust laws, each victory began with words. Without speech, action would have been crushed in silence. With speech, lies were exposed and power was challenged.

The Constitution of one means your voice is your constitution. You do not need an office, a title, or a license. You speak as a living man or woman. That is enough. When you speak in honor, your words carry the weight of truth. They cannot be erased by ridicule. They cannot be silenced by threat. They remain evidence of sovereignty.

The true power of the First Amendment is not found in courts or statutes. It is found in the courage of the individual who speaks when silence is demanded. Courts can twist words. Legislatures can write codes. Agencies can issue regulations. But when one man or woman speaks truth in honor, the illusion begins to collapse. The voice of one sovereign exposes the fraud of authority more effectively than any statute.

Officials know this, which is why they rely on intimidation. They send notices in threatening language. They use uniforms and badges to project authority. They tell you that you cannot speak unless you are licensed, unless you follow procedure, unless you remain within approved boundaries. All of this is designed to make you forget that the First Amendment is not a favor. It is a recognition that your voice cannot lawfully be silenced.

History offers countless reminders. In colonial America, assemblies were banned, newspapers were censored, and speakers were punished. Yet men and women continued to meet, print, and speak. Their persistence proved that speech does not come from rulers. It comes from life. Without those acts of defiance, independence would never have been declared.

The same is true in every generation. When injustice rises, speech is the first weapon of truth. The system fears speech because it spreads without permission. One voice becomes many. A single affidavit becomes evidence that cannot be ignored. Words travel faster than decrees.

They awaken the conscience of others. That is why tyrannies always begin with censorship. They know that speech is the seed of liberty.

The sovereign man or woman must also understand the role of responsibility. Speech in honor is not license to harm. To slander, to deceive, or to incite violence is to fall into dishonor. Sovereignty carries duty. Your words must reflect truth, not malice. When you speak in truth, you stand on unshakable ground. Lies crumble when challenged, but truth endures. That is why speech in honor is more powerful than any weapon. It cannot be lawfully punished, for no harm is caused.

The First Amendment also confirms that sovereignty belongs to the individual, not to institutions. Consider the press. In 1791, the press meant pamphlets, leaflets, and local newspapers produced by ordinary men and women. It did not mean giant corporations. The amendment was written to protect the people's voice in print, not to grant monopoly to media empires. Today, the right of the press is your right to publish, print, or broadcast your truth. No license is required, because the source of the right is life itself.

Petition is another forgotten weapon of the sovereign. To petition government is to place on record your grievances and demands. It is not begging for favors. It is declaring dishonor when officials fail in duty. When a petition is ignored, it is evidence that rulers have broken the covenant.

Silence in response is consent to your claim. This is why sovereign men and women use notices and affidavits. They are modern petitions that place truth on the record. Unrebutted, they stand as law.

Assembly is equally vital. A lone voice is strong, but many voices together are stronger. When men and women gather in peace, they form a living constitution. Their presence is proof that sovereignty is not isolated. It is shared. Governments fear such assemblies because they cannot control them without revealing tyranny. That is why permits and restrictions are imposed. Yet no permit is required for life to gather. The right to assemble is not granted by city hall. It belongs to you already.

The Constitution of one does not mean isolation. It means each man and woman carries sovereignty within. When they join together, they form a constitution of many. That is the living Republic. The First Amendment ensures that this union of voices cannot lawfully be silenced. Even when officials attempt to forbid assembly, the truth remains: the right existed before their decree and survives beyond it.

Remember also that silence is dangerous. The system thrives on your silence. When you do not rebut, you appear to agree. When you do not question, you appear to consent. That is why speech is a duty as well as a right. Each time you ask for proof, you place the burden back on the claimant.

Each time you issue a notice, you collapse presumption. Each time you speak in court, you reveal the fiction. Without speech, presumption stands. With speech, presumption falls.

The First Amendment therefore operates on two levels. On one level it restrains government. On the deeper level it reminds you that voice is the essence of sovereignty. To remain silent when truth must be spoken is to surrender. To speak in honor is to reclaim standing. Every sovereign must learn this balance. Speak truth, not anger. Speak calmly, not in rage. Speak with proof, not with empty words. In this way your speech is evidence of sovereignty.

Think again of the language: "Congress shall make no law." This is the strongest wording possible. It is absolute. It leaves no room for exception. Yet officials pretend otherwise. They write codes to limit speech, they punish assembly, they regulate religion. All of this is dishonor. The words of the amendment expose their fraud. By pointing to the text, you remind them that even their own system admits it has no power over your voice.

The Constitution of one means you do not wait for officials to honor this right. You honor it yourself. You speak when conscience demands it. You gather with others without fear. You publish your truth in any form you choose. You petition for redress when wronged. You live as though the amendment did not give you these powers but only confirmed them. Because that is the truth.

The path of sovereignty requires courage. You will face ridicule for speaking plainly. You will face threats for questioning authority. But each time you stand in truth, you weaken the illusion of control. Each time you speak in honor, you remind rulers that they govern only by consent. The First Amendment is your shield. Your voice is your sword. Together they prove that freedom begins with the spoken word of the sovereign.

This chapter has shown that the First Amendment is more than ink on parchment. It is the living proof that voice belongs to you alone. It is the testimony that no government can silence you lawfully. It is the reminder that speech, faith, assembly, and petition are expressions of life itself. As a sovereign man or woman, you are the Constitution of one. The Bill of Rights does not hand you speech. It witnesses that you already hold it.

Chapter 3: The Second Amendment – The Right to Defend

The right to defend life is as old as life itself. Long before governments, courts, or armies, every man and woman carried the natural power to protect themselves, their families, and their homes. No king gave this right. No legislature created it. It flows from survival, from conscience, from the Creator.

The Second Amendment of the Bill of Rights is often debated, but its meaning is simple. It states: "A well regulated Militia, being necessary to the security of a free State, the right of the people to keep and bear Arms shall not be infringed." These words confirm a truth older than the nation. They testify that defense belongs to the people, not to rulers.

Notice again the language. It does not grant a right. It recognizes one. "Shall not be infringed" is the key. The amendment admits openly that the right already existed and that government has no authority to limit it. This is consistent with every other amendment. The Bill of Rights restrains rulers. It does not create privileges.

To bear arms is more than owning tools of defense. It is a symbol of sovereignty. An unarmed population is dependent. It must beg for protection. It cannot stand as equal to authority. An armed people, by contrast, are sovereign.

They carry proof that defense is not outsourced to officials. It belongs to them by birth. That is why rulers fear the Second Amendment. It places power in the hands of the people, where it belongs.

The phrase "well regulated Militia" has been twisted by officials to suggest that only state-controlled forces hold the right to arms. This is deception. In the language of the eighteenth century, "well regulated" meant well practiced, well prepared, well equipped. It did not mean controlled by government. And "Militia" did not mean the National Guard. It meant the people themselves, every able-bodied man and woman who could defend their community. The militia was not separate from the people. It was the people.

This truth is uncomfortable for those who seek control. They prefer a monopoly on force. They want the people dependent on police, armies, and agencies. They argue that safety requires disarmament. But history proves the opposite. Safety collapses when only rulers are armed. Tyranny always follows. From ancient empires to modern dictatorships, the first act of oppression is to disarm the population. Once the people cannot defend themselves, resistance becomes almost impossible.

The sovereign man or woman understands that defense is not optional. It is duty. To defend life, family, and community is responsibility. The right to bear arms is not about sport or recreation, though it includes those.

It is about survival and sovereignty. Without it, all other rights can be erased by force. With it, the people remain equal to authority.

Think of the maxim: no man is obliged to accept a benefit against his will. Police protection is offered as a benefit. But if you rely solely on police, you surrender your duty to defend. You accept dependency. True sovereignty refuses dependency. You hold the tools of defense yourself. You stand as protector first. That is what the Second Amendment affirms.

The wording "the security of a free State" also deserves attention. The amendment does not speak of the security of a government. It speaks of the security of a free State, which means the people themselves in their sovereign condition. The State is not the federal corporation in Washington. The State is the union of living men and women who stand free. Their security depends on their arms, not on government armies.

Today officials attempt to regulate this right into oblivion. They pass codes, licenses, and restrictions. They demand permits to purchase, register, or carry. They ban certain tools and dictate conditions. Each of these acts is unlawful because it infringes what was declared untouchable. The amendment says "shall not be infringed." There are no exceptions. Every restriction is dishonor.

The Constitution of one recognizes that the right to defend exists even if every statute is repealed or ignored. Paper cannot erase it. Disarmament cannot erase it. Confiscation cannot erase it.

The right remains because it flows from life. A man stripped of tools still holds the right. A woman attacked still holds the right. The Creator gave this right and no ruler can take it.

The sovereign perspective also reveals that arms are not limited to weapons of a certain era. The right to defend evolves with technology. Just as speech adapts from pamphlets to digital networks, defense adapts from muskets to modern tools. The principle remains constant: the people must have equal means to protect themselves. Government cannot lawfully demand that the people remain weak while it arms itself with the latest technology. Equality in defense is the very definition of security for a free State.

Stories of resistance confirm this truth. Throughout history, when communities were armed, tyranny was resisted. When they were disarmed, tyranny triumphed. The founders knew this, which is why the Second Amendment was placed so prominently. They understood that paper promises mean little without the power to defend them. A right without defense is a suggestion. A right with defense is sovereignty.

The Constitution of one means that each man and woman carries this right within themselves. You do not wait for officials to approve your defense. You do not ask permission to protect your family. You do not surrender your safety to bureaucrats. You accept the responsibility yourself. That is sovereignty. That is freedom.

To understand the depth of the Second Amendment, you must see it not only as a right but as an obligation. Defense is not about aggression or conquest. It is about protection. It is about the duty every man and woman carries to safeguard life, family, and community. Sovereignty demands responsibility. Without defense, sovereignty becomes empty words. With defense, sovereignty becomes reality.

Officials today claim that the Second Amendment allows them to control the tools of defense through licenses and regulations. They pretend that the people's right depends on government approval. This is false. The text says clearly that the right "shall not be infringed." Infringe means to trespass, to encroach, to weaken. Every license is an infringement. Every permit is an infringement. Every ban is an infringement. The words leave no room for compromise.

The deception comes from redefining terms. Rulers say that arms mean only muskets from the eighteenth century. They say militia means only state-controlled units. They say regulation means restriction. None of these claims are true. Arms mean the tools of defense appropriate to the time. Militia means the people themselves. Regulation in its original sense meant order, preparation, practice. The amendment was never meant to limit. It was meant to secure.

Look at the logic of the founders. They had just fought a war of independence. They faced the most powerful empire of their age. They knew that standing armies were dangerous to liberty.

They knew that government power must be restrained. So they wrote into law that the people must remain armed and able to resist tyranny. To believe they intended for future governments to disarm the people is to ignore the entire context.

The Second Amendment is not about hunting. It is not about sport. It is about balance of power. It is about making sure that government cannot rise above the people. As long as the people remain armed, government knows it must rule by consent, not by force. Disarmament shifts that balance. It leaves the people dependent and vulnerable. That is why tyranny always begins with gun control.

History provides endless proof. In the twentieth century, regimes that disarmed their citizens quickly moved into oppression. Once the people were powerless, mass arrests, forced labor, and genocide followed. When the people held arms, rulers had to tread carefully. They had to negotiate. They had to respect boundaries. The armed population was a shield against absolute power.

The Constitution of one sees this truth clearly. You are not safe because government says so. You are safe because you accept responsibility for defense. You are not secure because officials carry weapons. You are secure because you carry your own. To surrender that responsibility is to surrender sovereignty itself.

Critics argue that defense is dangerous. They point to accidents, crimes, and misuse. But this argument ignores the foundation of sovereignty. Every right carries responsibility.

Speech can be abused, yet no one argues that speech should be banned. Religion can be twisted, yet no one argues that faith should be outlawed. The misuse of a right does not erase the right. It proves the need for honor and responsibility.

The sovereign man or woman understands this balance. To bear arms in honor means to respect life. It means never to harm without cause. It means never to use tools of defense for aggression. It means standing ready, not reckless. The dishonor of a few does not erase the honor of the many. To strip rights from all because of the actions of some is injustice.

Officials also argue that modern weapons are too powerful for private citizens. They say that government must hold superior force to ensure order. This is another deception. The Second Amendment was written precisely so the people would never be outmatched by their rulers. Technology changes, but principle remains. The people must always hold the means to defend themselves against tyranny. Otherwise the amendment is meaningless.

Think again about the words "security of a free State." This does not mean the security of politicians or agencies. It means the security of a sovereign people living free. That security cannot exist if the people are disarmed. Without arms, they are subjects. With arms, they are equals. The amendment ensures equality of power, which is the foundation of freedom.

The Constitution of one affirms that the right to defend does not end with the collective. It begins with the individual. You are the first guardian of your life. You are the protector of your family. You are the defender of your home. This duty cannot be outsourced to police or armies. They arrive after harm is done. Sovereignty requires prevention, not reaction. The armed sovereign prevents harm by being prepared.

The maxim of law applies: he who fails to deny agrees. If you accept disarmament in silence, you appear to consent. That consent becomes contract. The sovereign does not remain silent. He speaks. He refuses to surrender his right. He makes it clear that defense is not negotiable. This is not rebellion. It is standing in truth.

Examples across America show that armed communities remain stronger. Criminals avoid places where people are prepared to defend themselves. Officials treat citizens with more respect when they know the people are not dependent. The presence of arms changes the balance of power at every level. It reminds rulers that authority flows from the people, not the other way around.

The Second Amendment is therefore more than a legal clause. It is the living proof of sovereignty. It declares that defense belongs to the people, always and without exception. It is the shield that protects every other right. Without it, speech can be silenced, property can be seized, homes can be invaded, and courts can rule without fear of resistance. With it, every right stands stronger.

The Constitution of one recognizes this truth. You carry the right to defend within yourself. No license adds to it. No statute can erase it. It is part of your birth. The amendment is evidence, not source. To honor it is to accept responsibility for your own defense. To dishonor it is to surrender sovereignty to rulers who do not have your best interest at heart.

In the end, the Second Amendment speaks not to government but to you. It says clearly: your right to defend shall not be infringed. It is your duty to remember this, to live it, and to pass it on. A free people must remain armed. A sovereign man or woman must remain prepared. This is the balance of liberty. This is the Constitution of one.

Chapter 4: The Third Amendment – Home as Castle

The home is sacred. It is the place where life is lived in peace, where family gathers, where privacy is honored, and where sovereignty is most visible. No authority is greater inside a home than the living man or woman who dwells there. The Third Amendment of the Bill of Rights affirms this truth in simple words: "No Soldier shall, in time of peace be quartered in any house, without the consent of the Owner, nor in time of war, but in a manner to be prescribed by law."

At first glance, some dismiss this amendment as outdated. They say it applied only to the 1700s, when British troops were forced upon colonists. But the principle is timeless. It declares that the home is not property of the state. It declares that rulers cannot impose themselves into private life. It declares that every man and woman is sovereign within their dwelling.

The phrase "without the consent of the Owner" is the key. Consent makes law. If you do not consent, no lawful quartering can take place. This principle extends beyond soldiers. It applies to all intrusions. No official has authority to invade your home without consent, unless a true crime of harm, loss, or fraud has been committed and due process has been honored. The amendment is a clear rejection of forced intrusion.

Think of the maxim: every man's house is his castle. This principle existed long before the United States. English common law recognized it centuries earlier. The founders included it in the Bill of Rights because they knew that without protection of the home, all liberty collapses. If the state can enter, occupy, and control your dwelling, then you are no longer free. You are a tenant of rulers, not an owner in sovereignty.

The Constitution of one affirms that the home reflects the sovereign himself. To enter without consent is to trespass upon the living. To quarter soldiers, agents, or officials is to declare that the individual has no authority. That is why the Third Amendment is vital. It tells the government that the home is off limits without consent.

Though the amendment speaks of soldiers, the principle applies more broadly. Today the threats to the home come in new forms. Surveillance devices, forced inspections, property codes, and regulatory searches all attempt to bypass consent. Officials claim authority to enter for health, safety, or zoning. But the sovereign perspective reminds us: the home is a castle. Entry without consent is dishonor unless supported by true due process.

Consider the difference between a warrant supported by probable cause and an administrative inspection. A warrant, when lawfully issued, is supposed to respond to a specific harm or crime. An inspection, by contrast, assumes authority without harm. The first may be justified if natural law is broken. The second is intrusion without consent. The Third Amendment spirit rejects such intrusions. It says clearly that rulers cannot treat homes as their own.

This principle is more important today than ever. Governments expand surveillance, deploy technology, and seek to regulate every corner of life. They act as though ownership is conditional. But the Third Amendment stands as evidence that ownership is absolute. Consent is required. Without consent, intrusion is unlawful.

The Constitution of one recognizes that sovereignty begins at the threshold of the home. You are sovereign in your body, and that sovereignty extends outward to your dwelling. To surrender your home is to surrender your independence. That is why rulers seek property taxes, permits, and inspections. They want you to believe you are only a tenant, not an owner. The Third Amendment exposes this lie.

Even in times of crisis, the principle holds. The amendment allows quartering only in wartime and only according to law. That law must itself respect due process. It cannot erase the principle of consent. War does not abolish sovereignty. War does not erase the castle. Even under extreme conditions, the rights of the individual remain.

The story of America proves this. Colonists resisted British quartering not because of inconvenience but because of principle. To house soldiers without consent was to admit subjugation. It was proof that the king's claim outranked the sovereignty of the people.

By rejecting it, the colonists affirmed that liberty begins at home. The Third Amendment is the permanent testimony of that stand.

The maxim "a man's home is his castle" means more than privacy. It means jurisdiction. Within your home, you are the highest authority. No man can enter without your word. No official can claim superior standing. To protect the home is to protect the boundary between sovereign and state. Without that boundary, freedom becomes meaningless.

The Constitution of one teaches that the home is both symbol and reality of sovereignty. You feed your family there. You raise your children there. You keep your property there. You rest, recover, and think in that space. If rulers can invade it at will, then your life belongs to them. If they cannot, then your life remains your own. That is why the Third Amendment matters, even today.

When you see the home as a castle, you begin to understand the true weight of the Third Amendment. It is not about military housing. It is about authority. It is about whether the living man or woman is master of their own dwelling or whether they live at the pleasure of the state. Every intrusion without consent is a challenge to sovereignty. Every assertion of ownership by government is a denial of liberty.

Consider modern property law. You pay taxes on your home each year. If you fail to pay, the state threatens to seize the property. What does this reveal? It shows that the state sees itself as the true owner and you as a tenant. But the Third Amendment reminds us that ownership rests with the living. Consent cannot be forced through threat. True ownership means the right to exclude others, including the government.

Surveillance technology is a new form of quartering. Cameras on poles, devices that scan your home, and data collection by agencies all amount to the presence of authority in your private space. No soldier may be physically in your house, yet their electronic eye is there. The principle is the same. Sovereignty is diminished when the state inserts itself into your home life without your consent. The Third Amendment's spirit condemns such actions.

The maxim of law applies: he who enters another's property without right is a trespasser. This maxim is not suspended by technology. The same truth holds whether the trespasser is a soldier at the door or a camera in the sky. Your consent is required. Without it, the act is dishonor.

Look also at administrative searches. Officials claim the power to enter homes to check on building codes, safety rules, or welfare concerns. These are modern versions of forced quartering. They assume the state has a superior claim to your dwelling. But the Constitution of one denies that presumption. No man has authority over another's home without clear proof of harm. Inspections without injury are intrusions without consent.

The Third Amendment also speaks to the principle of peace. It says no soldier shall be quartered in time of peace. That phrase is vital.

Peace means no justification for intrusion. Peace means rulers must remain outside unless invited. Today governments act as though perpetual emergency justifies their presence. They claim crisis after crisis to excuse intrusion. But the amendment shows that peace is the natural state. Intrusion must remain the rare exception, not the norm.

From a sovereign perspective, the home is more than shelter. It is jurisdiction. Within its walls you are judge, protector, and authority. To allow intrusion without consent is to hand over that jurisdiction. It is to surrender sovereignty at the threshold. That is why tyrants target the home. They know that to control a people they must control their dwellings. Seizing homes, quartering troops, and taxing property are all tools of domination. The Third Amendment exists to prevent this.

Think again of the phrase "without the consent of the Owner." This places the highest authority in your hands. Consent cannot be forced. Consent cannot be assumed. Consent must be freely given. If it is not, quartering is unlawful. This principle extends beyond soldiers to every demand of the state. When an officer demands entry, the question is not what code he cites but whether you consent. Without consent, he has no lawful standing.

History proves the power of this principle. When colonists resisted British quartering acts, they were not only protecting their space. They were affirming sovereignty. They understood that to allow soldiers inside was to admit subjugation.

By refusing, they declared independence before the Declaration itself was signed. The Third Amendment is the written record of that refusal.

The Constitution of one applies this truth today. You are the gatekeeper of your home. You decide who enters. You decide what conditions apply. No statute overrides your consent. No policy erases your authority. When you remember this, fear fades. You stop thinking of yourself as a tenant of government. You stand as an owner, as sovereign, as master of your own castle.

This does not mean you live in isolation. Sovereignty is not lawlessness. It is order based on honor. You may welcome guests, allow neighbors, or invite officials if you choose. But the choice must always be yours. That is the line that separates freedom from servitude. When choice disappears, when consent is assumed, sovereignty is lost.

The Third Amendment is therefore a shield against more than quartering. It is a shield against every intrusion without consent. It stands against taxes that treat you as tenant. It stands against surveillance that treats you as suspect. It stands against inspections that treat you as incompetent. It declares that the living man or woman, in their home, is sovereign.

To live this truth requires courage. Officials may resist. They may threaten with codes and statutes. They may insist that ownership is conditional. But each time you stand in honor, you remind them of the truth. You remind them that the amendment binds them, not you.

You remind them that the home is sacred, that sovereignty begins at the threshold, and that consent is king.

The maxim "every man's house is his castle" is not a figure of speech. It is law. It is principle. It is the lived reality of sovereignty. The Third Amendment affirms it for all time. You need no further proof. You are the owner. You are the sovereign. You are the Constitution of one within your walls.

Chapter 5: The Fourth Amendment – The Right to Be Left Alone

The heart of sovereignty is the right to be left alone. No principle is more central to freedom than the ability to live in peace without unwanted intrusion. The Fourth Amendment of the Bill of Rights recognizes this truth. It states: "The right of the people to be secure in their persons, houses, papers, and effects, against unreasonable searches and seizures, shall not be violated, and no Warrants shall issue, but upon probable cause, supported by Oath or affirmation, and particularly describing the place to be searched, and the persons or things to be seized."

These words are powerful because they affirm privacy as sovereignty. To be secure in your person means your body cannot be violated without lawful cause. To be secure in your house means your home remains a castle. To be secure in your papers means your contracts, letters, and records belong to you. To be secure in your effects means your property cannot be seized without lawful process. All of these protections are rooted in one principle: consent is required before authority can act.

The framers wrote this amendment because they had lived under tyranny. British agents issued general warrants called writs of assistance. These allowed officials to search homes, seize property, and harass colonists without specific cause.

The colonists knew this was dishonor. It violated natural law. It treated men and women as subjects instead of sovereigns. The Fourth Amendment was written to prevent that abuse forever.

Notice again the structure. The amendment does not grant rights. It restrains rulers. It says the right "shall not be violated." That language is absolute. It leaves no room for assumption. It declares that government cannot invade your privacy without proof of cause and without particular description. Broad authority is forbidden.

The sovereign man or woman recognizes that privacy is not a gift. It is a birthright. You are not required to share your body, your home, your papers, or your property with anyone unless you consent. Government intrusion must meet the highest standard because intrusion is dishonor. Probable cause is the minimum proof required, and even that must be supported by oath or affirmation. Without it, entry is trespass.

Think of the maxim: he who asserts must prove. If an officer claims authority to search, he must show the warrant. If a clerk claims power to seize property, he must show lawful order. If no such proof exists, the claim collapses. Without proof, consent is assumed. That is why silence is dangerous. That is why the sovereign must speak and demand evidence.

The Fourth Amendment also exposes the fraud of modern surveillance. Officials pretend that watching, recording, or collecting data does not count as a search.

They use technology to bypass consent. They gather information on phones, computers, and networks without warrants. Yet the principle remains. To monitor without consent is to search. To collect data without permission is to seize. The tools may change, but the dishonor is the same.

The Constitution of one insists that privacy is sacred. Your body, your home, your papers, and your effects are extensions of your sovereignty. They are not open to inspection by default. They are not subject to fishing expeditions. They are yours by right. Government may act only when lawful cause is proven and described in detail. Anything less is intrusion without consent.

History shows that rulers fear privacy. They fear the people being left alone because privacy creates independence. An independent man or woman cannot be easily controlled. That is why surveillance grows. That is why searches expand. Dependency requires intrusion. Sovereignty requires separation. The Fourth Amendment draws that line.

But the amendment is only evidence. The true source of privacy is life itself. You did not need paper to know that your body belongs to you. You did not need parchment to know that your home is private. You did not need ink to know that your property is yours. These truths were obvious before 1791. The amendment is testimony, not creation.

The sovereign perspective demands vigilance. Intrusion is constant. Officials will always test boundaries. They will claim emergency.

They will claim safety. They will claim necessity. These are excuses to bypass consent. The sovereign man or woman must stand firm. You ask for proof. You refuse assumption. You remind officials that privacy is your default condition.

The maxim of law states that no one is obliged to accept a benefit against his will. Government often frames intrusion as benefit. Surveillance is said to provide safety. Searches are said to provide protection. Seizures are said to provide order. But benefits imposed without consent are dishonor. True safety arises from sovereignty, not from forced intrusion.

The Fourth Amendment is therefore more than protection against police abuse. It is recognition of the principle that you are sovereign over your space and property. To forget this is to accept slavery disguised as safety. To remember it is to reclaim the right to be left alone.

The promise of the Fourth Amendment is not complicated. It is the guarantee that the state must leave you alone unless it can prove lawful cause. Yet the system works tirelessly to erode this promise. Each new statute, each new regulation, each new surveillance program is an attempt to shift the burden away from proof and onto presumption. Officials want the default to be intrusion, not privacy. Sovereignty demands the opposite. Privacy must be the default. Intrusion must be the rare exception.

Look at how the wording demands specificity. Warrants must describe the place to be searched and the persons or things to be seized. This requirement destroys the idea of general warrants. It means no fishing expeditions. It means no broad authority. It means every intrusion must be tied to a particular cause. Without that cause and description, a search is void. This principle is simple, yet it is ignored by agencies that sweep up data on millions without particularity. The amendment stands as evidence against them.

The sovereign man or woman must remember that technology does not erase principle. Whether officials break down a door or scan your computer, the rule is the same. Without probable cause, supported by oath, and describing the specific target, intrusion is unlawful. To accept otherwise is to allow rulers to redefine words until liberty vanishes. The amendment does not permit such redefinition. It restrains.

Think of your body. To be secure in your person means that government cannot lawfully seize you, test you, or search you without probable cause. Yet statutes today allow stops, searches, and tests without warrants. These are unlawful, even if judges approve them. A court cannot erase a birthright. A statute cannot override natural law. The Fourth Amendment echoes this truth. Your body is yours. Consent must be given before any intrusion.

Think of your home. The maxim says every man's house is his castle. The Fourth Amendment affirms this maxim. To enter without warrant is trespass.

To seize property without cause is theft. Yet property codes and regulatory searches happen daily. They are justified as safety measures, but safety does not erase consent. A safe society is one where homes are respected, not invaded.

Think of your papers. In the eighteenth century this meant letters, ledgers, and contracts. Today it includes digital files, messages, and records. The principle remains. Papers belong to you. They are your private effects. They cannot be seized or searched without cause. Yet agencies claim authority to read messages, track movements, and scan databases. These are seizures by another name. The amendment stands against them.

The sovereign perspective asks simple questions. Who is the injured party? Where is the contract binding me to inspection? What probable cause has been sworn under oath? If no answer is given, the search is dishonor. The act collapses when exposed to truth. That is why officials prefer silence. They hope you will comply without question. They hope you will accept intrusion as normal.

Silence is consent. If you do not object, intrusion appears lawful. That is why the sovereign must speak. You do not need anger or aggression. You need clarity. You say, "Where is the warrant? Where is the oath? What is the probable cause?" These questions shift the burden back to the claimant. If no proof is produced, the presumption falls.

The Constitution of one recognizes that the right to be left alone extends beyond paper. It is not limited to courtrooms or statutes. It is a principle of life. You live free because your space is yours. You live sovereign because your property is secure. You live in honor because you respect the same right in others. This balance is natural law. Harm no one. Take nothing. Respect privacy. Expect the same in return.

The Fourth Amendment is often ignored in practice, but that does not erase its truth. It remains evidence for you to use. It remains testimony that even rulers once admitted they must be restrained. It is a tool for the sovereign to expose dishonor. Each time you invoke it, you remind officials of their limits. Each time you demand proof, you weaken assumption.

Living this truth requires courage. Intrusion has become habit in modern society. Cameras on every street. Agents at every border. Data collected at every purchase. People accept this because they are told it is for safety. But safety without freedom is slavery. A cage may be safe, but it is still a cage. The sovereign chooses freedom, not cages.

To be left alone is not isolation. It is independence. It is the ability to decide when to share and when to close the door. It is the power to invite guests freely instead of being forced to host intruders. It is the dignity of ownership, of privacy, of sovereignty. That is what the Fourth Amendment affirms.

The maxim of law says that power given for protection cannot be used for oppression. Government claims to protect, but when it violates privacy it oppresses. That is dishonor. The sovereign must never forget this. Officials may wear badges, carry weapons, or sit on benches, but none of these symbols erase your birthright to be left alone.

The chapter closes with a reminder: the right to be secure is yours already. The Fourth Amendment is only the record. The true constitution is you. When you demand to be left alone, you live sovereignty. When you guard your privacy, you live freedom. When you respect the privacy of others, you live in honor. This is the Constitution of one in practice.

Chapter 6: The Fifth Amendment – No Man Bound Without Consent

The Fifth Amendment is one of the clearest proofs that sovereignty begins with the individual. It says: "No person shall be held to answer for a capital, or otherwise infamous crime, unless on a presentment or indictment of a Grand Jury, except in cases arising in the land or naval forces, or in the Militia, when in actual service in time of War or public danger; nor shall any person be subject for the same offence to be twice put in jeopardy of life or limb; nor shall be compelled in any criminal case to be a witness against himself; nor be deprived of life, liberty, or property, without due process of law; nor shall private property be taken for public use, without just compensation."

This long sentence carries within it the entire philosophy of consent. It affirms that no man or woman can be forced into obligation without clear proof, without process, without fairness. It restrains rulers from binding the sovereign through presumption. It is a shield against compelled speech, against double punishment, against seizure of property, and against deprivation of liberty without due process.

The phrase "no person shall be compelled in any criminal case to be a witness against himself" is central. It means the sovereign cannot be forced to speak against his own interest. Your silence cannot lawfully be used as evidence of guilt. To compel confession is dishonor. It violates the principle that consent must be freely given.

If words are forced, they are void. The amendment affirms that sovereignty protects your voice as well as your property.

The protection against double jeopardy is equally vital. To try a man twice for the same offence is to admit that the first trial failed. It is to harass, to punish without end, to treat the sovereign as property of the state. The amendment bars this dishonor. Once acquitted, the sovereign cannot be dragged back into the same battle. Finality is part of justice.

The requirement of due process is the heart of the Fifth Amendment. To deprive a man of life, liberty, or property without process is theft. Process means fair notice, impartial hearing, opportunity to be heard, and proof beyond assumption. Without process, rulers act in tyranny. With process, they are forced to prove their claim. The maxim holds: he who asserts must prove. Due process is the system's reluctant acknowledgment of that maxim.

The takings clause, which bars property seizure without just compensation, also reflects the principle of consent. Property belongs to the individual. If it is taken for public use, the owner must be compensated. This is not a favor. It is recognition that ownership cannot be erased by decree. To seize without compensation is theft, plain and simple.

The Constitution of one sees the Fifth Amendment as more than legal procedure. It is a statement that no man is bound without his consent. You cannot be forced to testify against yourself.

You cannot be punished twice for the same act. You cannot be deprived of property without process and compensation. Each of these protections rests on the idea that sovereignty belongs to the individual, not the state.

Think of how this plays out in daily life. Officials send notices demanding payment. They presume you are a debtor. They treat silence as guilt. The Fifth Amendment stands as evidence that you cannot be compelled to testify against yourself. You are not bound to confirm their claim. They must prove it. Your silence is not confession. It is standing in sovereignty.

Consider also the way property is seized today through forfeiture statutes. Agencies claim authority to take homes, cars, or money suspected of being linked to crime. Often no conviction is required. This is pure dishonor. It violates the Fifth Amendment directly. No property may be taken without process and without compensation. The sovereign man or woman knows this and demands proof. Without it, the seizure is theft under color of law.

The Fifth Amendment also shows why statutes are contracts. You are not bound by them without consent. If officials wish to bind you, they must follow process. They must show agreement. They must prove obligation. Without such proof, their demand collapses. The amendment restrains them from forcing you into contract by presumption.

The maxim of law "consent makes the law" applies here more than anywhere else. You cannot be bound without knowing agreement. You cannot be punished without process. You cannot be compelled to act against yourself. Sovereignty means responsibility for your words and your silence. To speak in honor is powerful. To remain silent in honor is equally powerful. Both are choices of the sovereign.

This is why rulers fear the Fifth Amendment. They prefer a system where silence is guilt, where property is seized without trial, where confessions are extracted under threat. They prefer a system where process is bypassed in the name of efficiency. But the amendment exposes their fraud. It testifies that sovereignty cannot be erased by speed or convenience.

The deeper truth of the Fifth Amendment is that it makes government admit its limits. It tells rulers that they cannot move against the sovereign without meeting strict conditions. They cannot presume guilt. They cannot seize property by decree. They cannot silence you and then use your silence as proof. They must prove every claim with evidence, oath, and process. This is not a grant of privilege. It is a recognition that the sovereign stands above the state unless he consents to be bound.

Take the example of compelled testimony. In many countries men and women are forced to confess under threat, torture, or coercion. The founders knew this was dishonor. They wrote into the Bill of Rights that no person shall be compelled to be a witness against himself.

This protection is not limited to courts. It extends to every demand for confession, signature, or admission. When an agency sends you forms and demands that you admit obligation, the Fifth Amendment affirms that you cannot be compelled. You are free to refuse without penalty because no man is bound without consent.

The concept of due process has been twisted over time, but its essence remains. Due process means fairness rooted in natural law. It means notice of the claim. It means the right to confront the accuser. It means the opportunity to answer in honor. It means a fair tribunal. Without these, there is no lawful deprivation of life, liberty, or property. Many officials act as though due process is a box to check, a ritual to perform. The sovereign knows it is more. It is the line between liberty and tyranny.

The clause protecting property from seizure without just compensation also reflects this principle. To take property without paying is theft, no matter what words are used. Taxation without consent, forfeiture without conviction, and eminent domain without fair value all violate this truth. Sovereignty demands that property is respected because property is an extension of the individual. To seize it is to wound the sovereign. Compensation is not charity. It is acknowledgment that ownership belongs first to the people.

Consider double jeopardy. This principle says that once acquitted, you cannot be tried again for the same act. Without this rule, rulers could drag a man into court endlessly until he broke.

Double jeopardy protection is recognition that the sovereign cannot be harassed without end. It forces government to prove its claim once and only once. It prevents the abuse of endless trials as punishment.

The Fifth Amendment also shows how silence can be a shield. When questioned by officials, many believe they must answer. They fear that silence will be seen as guilt. In truth, silence in honor is protection. You cannot be compelled to incriminate yourself. You do not have to provide evidence against your own standing. The burden of proof lies with the accuser. Your role is to demand proof, not to supply it.

The maxim of law says that the burden of proof is on the one who affirms, not on the one who denies. The Fifth Amendment is the written form of that maxim. It protects the sovereign from being tricked into self-condemnation. It forces rulers to stand on their own claims. Without this principle, every man would be bound by his own fear and every woman by her own words under pressure. The amendment breaks that chain.

Look also at the phrase "without due process of law." Many believe this phrase means statutes written by legislatures. In truth, process of law means process consistent with natural law. It means lawful judgment by peers, not by officials. It means fairness, not presumption. When due process is replaced by administrative procedure, the result is not law but policy. The sovereign must reject policies that bypass true process.

The Fifth Amendment is therefore not a technicality. It is a shield against presumption. It affirms that you cannot be bound without consent, confession, or proven harm. It reminds rulers that their power ends where your sovereignty begins. It is testimony that the living man or woman stands above paper fiction.

The Constitution of one interprets this amendment as a personal covenant. It says that you do not surrender your life, liberty, or property by silence or ignorance. You stand in honor. You refuse to be compelled. You demand due process. You refuse to be tried twice. You protect your property from seizure without compensation. Each of these choices is sovereignty in action.

The chapter closes with a truth the system wants forgotten. The Fifth Amendment is not about protecting criminals. It is about protecting the sovereign. It is not a loophole. It is a wall against tyranny. It is the acknowledgment that consent is required before any man can be bound. Without it, liberty dies. With it, sovereignty lives.

Chapter 7: The Sixth Amendment – The Jury as Shield

The Sixth Amendment speaks to the power of the people themselves to act as the highest court of justice. It declares: "In all criminal prosecutions, the accused shall enjoy the right to a speedy and public trial, by an impartial jury of the State and district wherein the crime shall have been committed, which district shall have been previously ascertained by law, and to be informed of the nature and cause of the accusation; to be confronted with the witnesses against him; to have compulsory process for obtaining witnesses in his favor, and to have the Assistance of Counsel for his defence."

These words establish the jury as a shield between the individual and the state. The accused is not to be judged by officials, but by peers. The trial is not to be hidden, but open to the public. The accusation is not to be vague, but clear. Witnesses must appear in person, not through rumor. Evidence must be confronted, not assumed. The accused must have the chance to call witnesses and to receive help in defense. Every part of this amendment restrains rulers and empowers the people.

The jury is one of the most powerful expressions of sovereignty. It embodies the principle that authority rests with the people, not the state. Judges may sit in robes, prosecutors may present charges, but it is the jury that decides guilt or innocence. That power belongs to the community. It is not delegated from the government. It is reserved by the people.

This principle is rooted in natural law. Justice is not served when a man is judged by his accusers. Justice requires impartial judgment by equals. In tribes and communities across history, disputes were settled by peers. Elders or groups listened to both sides and made a fair decision. The jury system is simply a continuation of this principle. It prevents rulers from being both accuser and judge.

The sovereign perspective emphasizes one part of the jury's power that officials rarely admit: jury nullification. This is the power of a jury to refuse to convict under an unjust law. If the statute itself is dishonor, the jury may say no. This principle is ancient. It recognizes that statutes are not law unless the people consent. The jury holds the final authority. When twelve peers refuse to convict, the statute collapses.

Officials fear jury nullification. They instruct jurors to follow the law as the judge explains it, even if they disagree. They withhold the truth that jurors may vote their conscience. This is deception. The Sixth Amendment gives the right to a jury, not the duty to obey a judge. The jury's role is not to rubber-stamp statutes, but to deliver justice. Justice belongs to the people, not to officials.

The requirement of a speedy trial also reflects sovereignty. To hold a man indefinitely without judgment is tyranny. Rulers know that delay can destroy lives. The amendment restrains them. It forces them to move quickly or release the accused. Time is protection. Delay is dishonor. The sovereign must not be left in limbo.

The demand for public trials is equally important. Secret proceedings are the tools of tyranny. When trials are hidden, abuse thrives. The amendment requires openness. The people must see justice done. Public trials expose dishonor. They ensure accountability. They remind rulers that their actions are under the eyes of the community.

The right to know the cause of accusation is also central. Vague charges are traps. They leave the accused unable to defend. They allow rulers to harass without end. The amendment forbids this. Every accusation must be specific. The accused must know exactly what he faces. Without this, there is no justice.

The right to confront witnesses also protects sovereignty. Anonymous accusers and secret evidence are dishonor. The accused has the right to face those who speak against him. He has the right to test their words in open court. Without confrontation, lies prevail. With it, truth is revealed.

The right to compulsory process ensures balance. The accused may summon witnesses in his favor. This prevents one-sided trials. It ensures that the sovereign has equal power to present evidence. The trial must be fair, not a show staged by rulers.

Finally, the right to assistance of counsel confirms that defense is not a privilege. It is a necessity. No man should stand alone against the state without help if he desires it. But the sovereign also retains the right to defend himself. Counsel is an option, not an obligation. The choice belongs to the accused, not to officials.

The Constitution of one recognizes that the Sixth Amendment is not about technical procedure. It is about power. It places the final decision in the hands of peers, not rulers. It ensures transparency. It demands fairness. It allows conscience to prevail over statutes. It reminds government that justice flows from the people.

The deeper meaning of the Sixth Amendment lies in its recognition that the people themselves are the last line of defense against tyranny. The state may write statutes, employ judges, and field armies of prosecutors, but in the end guilt or innocence rests with ordinary men and women sitting as a jury. This power is rarely acknowledged openly because it places sovereignty directly in the hands of the people.

When a jury delivers a verdict, it is not simply deciding a case. It is exercising the authority of the community over the state. The accused is judged not by officials but by equals. That is sovereignty in action. This is why the system works so hard to mislead jurors. They are told their only job is to apply the law as given by the judge. They are told conscience and fairness must be set aside. This is a lie. The amendment does not say the accused shall be judged by officials. It says by an impartial jury. The jury holds the power to decide what justice requires.

Jury nullification flows directly from this truth. If a statute itself is unjust, the jury has the authority to refuse conviction. This power has been used throughout history. Juries refused to convict men and women who resisted slavery.

They refused to convict those accused of violating prohibition statutes. They refused to convict in cases where enforcement would have caused dishonor. Each time, the jury proved that sovereignty belongs to the people.

Officials fear this power because it undermines their control. If jurors knew the full truth, statutes could be nullified whenever the people judged them unjust. That is why courts forbid lawyers from mentioning nullification. That is why judges instruct juries to follow the law, even when it violates conscience. Yet no instruction can erase the sovereign power of the jury. Each juror holds it. Each juror may use it. It cannot be taken away.

The Sixth Amendment also protects against manipulation by requiring trials to be local. The accused must be judged by a jury from the state and district where the alleged crime occurred. This prevents rulers from dragging the accused to distant courts or hostile forums. It ensures judgment by neighbors and peers, not strangers chosen by authority. It roots justice in community, not in bureaucracy.

The right to a speedy trial has special importance for sovereignty. Time is a weapon in the hands of rulers. By delaying trial, they keep the accused in limbo, draining resources, reputation, and spirit. The amendment forces them to act quickly. It reminds them that freedom cannot be suspended without prompt proof. Delay without cause is dishonor. Sovereignty demands swiftness.

The requirement of public trials also guards against secret injustice. Tyranny thrives in the dark. Public trials ensure transparency. They place proceedings before the eyes of the community. They remind rulers that justice must be open to scrutiny. No man should be condemned in secret. The sovereign insists on light, not shadow.

The right to be informed of the accusation further affirms the principle of consent. You cannot consent to defend yourself if you do not know the claim. Vague charges are traps that keep the accused bound without clarity. The amendment forbids such vagueness. It demands specificity. The sovereign must know the exact cause in order to answer with honor.

Confronting witnesses is another shield. Anonymous testimony is dishonor because it prevents challenge. To face the accuser is to balance power. Without this, the accused is at the mercy of rumor. With it, lies crumble under cross-examination. The sovereign demands confrontation because truth cannot hide in the open.

Compulsory process for witnesses in favor ensures fairness. The accused is not left defenseless. He can summon those who will speak truth for him. The state cannot monopolize testimony. Balance is preserved. Justice requires both sides to be heard fully.

The assistance of counsel completes the circle. No man should be forced to face the machinery of the state without help if he seeks it. Yet this does not erase the right of self-defense.

The sovereign may choose to speak for himself. The state cannot force representation upon him. Counsel is a choice, not an obligation. Sovereignty means the decision is yours.

The Constitution of one views the Sixth Amendment as the living proof that justice belongs to the people. The jury is not a tool of the court. It is the conscience of the community. It stands as shield between ruler and ruled. It holds the power to nullify unjust statutes. It embodies the principle that law without consent is not law at all.

To serve as a juror is therefore not a burden but a duty of sovereignty. It is an opportunity to stand in honor, to refuse injustice, to defend liberty for another as you would want defended for yourself. Each juror is a sovereign in judgment. Together they form the shield of the community.

The Sixth Amendment is not a relic. It is alive each time a jury sits. It is alive each time a trial is public. It is alive each time an accusation is made clear. It is alive each time a witness is confronted. It is alive each time a man defends himself. The sovereign must remember this. Without juries, rulers would judge without restraint. With juries, rulers are bound by the people.

This chapter closes with a reminder: sovereignty is not isolated to the individual. It is shared in community. The jury proves this. When twelve peers stand together, they form a living wall against tyranny.

They declare by verdict that the people are the true authority. That is the Constitution of one multiplied into many. That is the Republic. That is freedom.

Chapter 8: The Seventh Amendment – Commerce and Common Law

The Seventh Amendment is one of the least discussed, yet it carries profound meaning for the sovereign man or woman. It declares: "In Suits at common law, where the value in controversy shall exceed twenty dollars, the right of trial by jury shall be preserved, and no fact tried by a jury, shall be otherwise reexamined in any Court of the United States, than according to the rules of the common law."

This short amendment affirms that disputes over property, contracts, and commerce must be judged not by officials but by juries under common law. It sets a bright line between statutory control and natural justice. It reminds rulers that when property is at stake, the people remain the final authority.

Notice the phrase "suits at common law." Common law is not the same as statutory law. Common law is rooted in custom, conscience, and natural principles. It asks only: was harm caused, was loss inflicted, was fraud committed. Statutory law, by contrast, is corporate policy. It creates obligations through registration and consent, not through injury. The Seventh Amendment affirms that disputes of substance belong to common law, not to statutes.

The threshold of twenty dollars may seem quaint today, but its meaning is profound. It declares that even small controversies require the protection of a jury. Property disputes are never trivial.

To seize even a small amount without consent is dishonor. By setting such a low bar, the amendment affirms that the principle matters more than the amount. The right of trial by jury cannot be denied simply because the value is modest.

The second half of the amendment is equally important. It says that no fact tried by a jury shall be reexamined in any court except according to the rules of common law. This binds judges. It prevents them from overturning jury verdicts by decree. It makes the jury the highest authority on fact. Once the people decide, the matter stands. That is sovereignty in action.

The Constitution of one sees the Seventh Amendment as a guard against the creeping power of statutory courts. Today most disputes are handled by administrative tribunals or corporate-style courts. They bypass juries. They rely on codes instead of common law. This is dishonor. It strips the people of their shield and replaces it with bureaucracy. The amendment exposes this fraud. It reminds us that property and contract belong under the authority of juries, not clerks.

The principle of common law is simple: do no harm, cause no loss, commit no fraud. Disputes arise when one man claims another has violated these principles. The role of the jury is to decide if that claim is true. Statutes add layers of regulation, licensing, and obligation. They shift focus from harm to paperwork. They trap people in contracts they never knowingly signed. The Seventh Amendment resists this by demanding that real controversies return to common law judgment.

Consider the maxim: no one is obliged to accept a benefit against his will. Many statutory obligations are framed as benefits. Licenses are sold as protections. Registrations are sold as conveniences. Taxes are sold as services. But when disputes arise, the question should not be whether the statute was followed. It should be whether harm, loss, or fraud occurred. That is the test of common law. The jury is the body that applies that test.

This is why officials avoid juries in civil disputes. They prefer administrative courts where decisions are made quickly by clerks. They argue that juries are slow, costly, or unnecessary. The real reason is control. Juries return power to the people. They bring conscience into the courtroom. They ask questions that statutes cannot answer. Did harm occur? Was loss caused? Was fraud proven? If not, the case collapses.

The Seventh Amendment preserves this shield. It keeps the jury at the center of civil justice. It prevents judges from overturning facts. It prevents rulers from bypassing the people. It ensures that property remains under the protection of community judgment.

The Constitution of one affirms that sovereignty extends into commerce. To contract is a natural right. To exchange goods, services, or property is part of life. But contracts must be voluntary. They must be honest. They must be free of fraud. Common law protects this truth. Statutes distort it. That is why the Seventh Amendment matters. It keeps commerce grounded in honor.

The Seventh Amendment is more than a procedural guarantee. It is a recognition that justice in commerce belongs to the people. Statutes are written to favor the state and its corporate partners. Common law exists to balance disputes fairly among equals. That is why the amendment protects jury trials in civil cases. It prevents rulers from monopolizing the field of commerce.

Think of how this principle applies to contracts. A true contract requires meeting of the minds, full disclosure, and mutual consent. If any element is missing, the contract is void. Common law recognizes this truth. Statutory courts, by contrast, often enforce contracts that were never truly agreed to. They assume consent from silence. They enforce adhesion contracts written in fine print. They treat the living man or woman as bound by paperwork they never understood. This is dishonor. The jury stands as the shield against it.

Consider property disputes. Under common law, ownership is simple. If you mix your labor with the land, the product is yours. If you buy or trade honestly, the property is yours. If someone takes it without consent, it is theft. Statutory law complicates this with endless regulations. It creates liens, taxes, and licenses that treat you as tenant instead of owner. When disputes arise, statutory courts side with the state. A jury under common law sees through the deception. It asks: who has rightful claim? Was there harm, loss, or fraud? Those questions restore honor.

The amendment's ban on reexamining jury facts is also crucial. Once a jury decides, the matter is settled. Judges cannot overturn verdicts simply because they dislike the outcome. This protects the sovereignty of the people. It ensures that rulers cannot erase community judgment with a wave of the hand. It binds courts to respect the conscience of jurors.

The Constitution of one reminds us that commerce itself is natural. People trade by instinct. They barter, exchange, and contract without rulers. Governments step in not to protect, but to control. They license trade, regulate exchange, and tax transactions. These acts are not protection. They are attempts to insert the state into private agreements. The Seventh Amendment affirms that disputes in commerce belong to juries, not to bureaucrats. It is evidence that the people remain the true authority.

Think of the maxim: he who does not deny, agrees. Statutory courts use this against people every day. If you fail to respond to a notice, they assume consent. If you fail to challenge a claim, they enforce it. But in a true common law jury trial, silence alone is not enough. Evidence must be presented. Harm must be proven. Fraud must be shown. The burden remains with the accuser. The jury ensures that presumption cannot replace proof.

Officials dislike this because it exposes the fragility of their system. Statutory power rests on assumption. Common law requires proof. A jury in conscience demands evidence. That is why rulers bypass juries whenever possible.

They create administrative tribunals where decisions are swift and unquestioned. They tell people it is more efficient. Efficiency is not justice. Justice requires peers, conscience, and fairness.

The Seventh Amendment also connects to property rights in a deeper sense. Property is more than land or goods. It is the fruit of your labor. To take it without consent is to enslave the worker. Common law respects this truth. Statutes ignore it. They create endless obligations that siphon property from the people to the state. When disputes arise, the jury restores balance. It sees the individual as owner, not as subject.

Examples from history confirm this. Juries have often sided with individuals against corporations. They have refused to enforce unjust contracts. They have awarded damages when fraud was proven. They have protected property against seizure. These cases show the continuing relevance of the Seventh Amendment. It is not an antique. It is a living shield.

For the sovereign man or woman, the amendment is also a reminder to demand jury trials when disputes arise. Administrative hearings are traps. They deny the protection of peers. They leave you at the mercy of officials. By demanding a jury, you reclaim standing. You insist on common law. You force the accuser to prove harm, loss, or fraud. This is sovereignty in practice.

The chapter closes with this truth: commerce and contracts are part of life, but they must be governed by honor, not control.

The Seventh Amendment affirms that the people remain the judges of such disputes. Juries under common law are the shield against corporate and statutory overreach. They ensure that sovereignty extends into commerce. They preserve the principle that no man or woman is bound without consent, and no property may be seized without proof.

The Constitution of one declares that the Seventh Amendment is not about twenty dollars. It is about freedom. It is about the right to have disputes judged by peers, not rulers. It is about keeping commerce honest. It is about ensuring that sovereignty governs property, not bureaucracy. It is about remembering that justice belongs to the people, always.

Chapter 9: The Eighth Amendment – Limits on Punishment

The Eighth Amendment is a direct barrier against cruelty, abuse, and financial exploitation by the state. It reads: "Excessive bail shall not be required, nor excessive fines imposed, nor cruel and unusual punishments inflicted." Though short in words, it speaks volumes about sovereignty and the limits of government power.

The amendment addresses three forms of abuse that rulers have always used to control populations. The first is bail, the second is fines, and the third is punishment. Each of these, if unchecked, can be turned into a weapon to enslave. The Eighth Amendment restrains these weapons. It affirms that sovereignty cannot be crushed under the weight of financial demands or physical torment.

Consider bail. In theory, bail is meant to ensure appearance in court. In practice, it has often been used as ransom. By setting bail at levels ordinary men and women cannot pay, rulers keep them imprisoned before any conviction. This is dishonor. It presumes guilt and punishes without trial. The Eighth Amendment forbids it by requiring that bail not be excessive. Bail must reflect fairness, not control. It must not be used as a tool to break the spirit of the accused.

Next consider fines. Fines are supposed to be proportionate to harm caused. But history shows rulers often impose massive fines for minor infractions.

They turn fines into revenue streams. They exploit the people under the guise of justice. This is dishonor. A fine that exceeds the nature of the offense is not justice. It is theft. The amendment forbids excessive fines for this reason. It reminds rulers that the sovereign is not a source of endless tribute.

Finally consider punishment. Cruel and unusual punishments are the hallmark of tyranny. Beatings, torture, executions by horrific methods, and endless confinement all serve to degrade the individual. They are designed to break the will and destroy sovereignty. The Eighth Amendment stands against this. It affirms that punishment must never be cruel. It must never be unusual. It must never be an act of vengeance by the state.

The Constitution of one interprets this amendment as a shield of dignity. The sovereign man or woman cannot be reduced to property through excessive financial demands. They cannot be broken through cruelty. They cannot be treated as less than human. The amendment reminds rulers that even in punishment, sovereignty remains.

Notice again the structure. The amendment does not grant rights. It restrains rulers. It binds them from excess. It limits their ability to exploit. The sovereign holds dignity as birthright. The amendment acknowledges it.

Think of the maxim: punishment should be corrective, not destructive. Natural law requires balance. If harm is done, restitution may be required. But cruelty exceeds balance.

Excessive fines exceed balance. Holding a man in jail before conviction through impossible bail exceeds balance. These acts are not lawful. They are oppression disguised as justice.

Modern systems have stretched punishment far beyond reason. Long prison terms for nonviolent acts, financial penalties that ruin families, and conditions that degrade rather than restore all violate the Eighth Amendment. Yet officials act as if statutes outrank the amendment. They impose dishonor and call it law. The sovereign must remember that true law is higher. The amendment is evidence that rulers know their limits, even if they ignore them.

Excessive bail reveals another principle: freedom is the default. A man is innocent until proven guilty. To cage him before conviction without cause is dishonor. Bail must be fair, accessible, and related to ensuring appearance. To set it beyond reach is to punish before judgment. This is unlawful. The amendment condemns it.

Excessive fines reveal how easily rulers slip into greed. Governments now treat fines as revenue. Parking tickets, traffic violations, administrative penalties, all are multiplied to feed the treasury. This is taxation by another name. It is extraction without consent. The Eighth Amendment is evidence against it. Sovereignty demands that no fine exceed the harm caused. Anything beyond that is theft.

Cruel and unusual punishments reveal the dark side of unchecked power. History is filled with rulers who tortured to create fear. Even today prisons use solitary confinement, degrading conditions, and endless sentences. These practices are cruelty disguised as justice. The sovereign sees through this. Punishment must correct, not destroy. It must honor dignity, not erase it.

The Constitution of one declares that punishment belongs within natural law. If harm is done, restitution restores balance. If fraud is committed, truth corrects it. If peace is broken, order must be rebuilt. None of these require cruelty. None require excess. They require honor. The Eighth Amendment affirms this truth.

The Eighth Amendment does not abolish punishment. It restrains it. It demands that even when judgment is rendered, the dignity of the sovereign man or woman must remain. Punishment without restraint is vengeance. Punishment with restraint is justice. That balance is the mark of honor.

Take the example of bail again. The purpose of bail is simple: to ensure that the accused returns to court. Yet in many cases, bail is set at levels impossible for ordinary people. This practice converts bail into a weapon. It turns the presumption of innocence into pretrial punishment. The sovereign perspective rejects this entirely. Bail must reflect fairness. If it becomes impossible, it ceases to be bail and becomes imprisonment without conviction. That is dishonor, and it is unlawful.

Now look at fines. A fine that exceeds the harm done is not lawful restitution. It is exploitation. When a government uses fines to fund itself, it confesses its dishonor. Sovereignty demands balance. If a man damages another's property, he should restore it. If a woman causes loss, she should make it whole. That is lawful. But when fines are multiplied beyond reason, when penalties for minor acts reach thousands of dollars, it is theft by decree. The Eighth Amendment was written to prevent such abuses.

Cruel and unusual punishments expose the deepest corruption of authority. When rulers inflict torment to instill fear, they treat the sovereign as livestock. They seek not justice but domination. Solitary confinement, endless imprisonment for minor offenses, and degrading conditions are all forms of cruelty. They strip the individual of dignity and destroy the soul. This is dishonor. The amendment stands as evidence that such practices are unlawful.

The Constitution of one recognizes that natural law provides the true guide for punishment. The principle is simple: restore balance. If harm is caused, repair it. If peace is broken, restore it. If fraud is committed, correct it. These remedies heal rather than destroy. They affirm the dignity of all involved. Cruelty and excess do the opposite. They deepen harm and spread dishonor.

Excessive bail, fines, and punishments also reveal a deeper fraud. They show that the system views people as property. When fines are multiplied, the individual is seen as a revenue source.

When bail is set impossibly high, the individual is seen as collateral. When punishments degrade, the individual is seen as disposable. This perspective denies sovereignty. It reduces the living man or woman to numbers on a ledger. The Eighth Amendment is testimony against this fraud.

History provides many warnings. Tyrannies of the past used cruel punishments to control populations. They branded, mutilated, and executed in ways designed to inspire terror. These acts did not bring justice. They brought obedience through fear. The founders knew this history. They wrote the Eighth Amendment to place a wall between the people and such cruelty. That wall remains, though officials often try to scale it.

For the sovereign, the amendment is more than words. It is a reminder that dignity must always be preserved. Even when accused, even when judged, even when punished, the individual remains sovereign. The state cannot lawfully destroy what it did not create. The body, the spirit, the dignity of the living man or woman remain beyond the reach of statutes.

The maxim of law says that equity abhors oppression. Excess is oppression. Cruelty is oppression. Unpayable fines are oppression. The Eighth Amendment affirms this maxim in writing. It stands as a witness that rulers must act with balance or admit dishonor.

The amendment also connects to other protections in the Bill of Rights. The Fourth guards privacy. The Fifth demands due process.

The Sixth gives trial by jury. The Seventh protects property disputes. The Eighth then ensures that when punishment comes, it is not turned into tyranny. Together these protections form a circle around the sovereign. Each one is a shield. The Eighth ensures that even in defeat, the individual is not destroyed.

The Constitution of one views this amendment as a covenant of honor. It says that rulers must never forget the humanity of the accused. It says that punishment must never exceed balance. It says that justice must never become cruelty. These principles are eternal. They are not bound to parchment. They are written in conscience. The amendment is only testimony. The true law is natural law.

This chapter closes with a truth that cannot be denied. Punishment is not license to abuse. Bail is not license to imprison. Fines are not license to steal. Sovereignty remains even when judgment is rendered. The Eighth Amendment affirms that dignity cannot be erased by decree. The sovereign man or woman carries this dignity always. It cannot be taken. It can only be dishonored by those who pretend authority.

Chapter 10: The Ninth Amendment – Rights Beyond Writing

The Ninth Amendment is one of the most revealing statements in the entire Bill of Rights. It reads: "The enumeration in the Constitution, of certain rights, shall not be construed to deny or disparage others retained by the people."

These few words carry a message that cuts through centuries of deception. They declare openly that your rights are not limited to those listed on parchment. They admit that rights exist beyond the page. They affirm that the Constitution itself is not the source of freedom, but merely a witness to it.

The framers knew that some would argue that only written rights were real rights. To prevent that deception, they wrote the Ninth Amendment. It is their confession that the list is incomplete, that liberty cannot be contained in ink. The rights of the people extend beyond what government chose to write down.

This principle is the essence of the Constitution of one. Freedom is not limited by text. It is as broad as life itself. You do not need a line in the Bill of Rights to know that you have the right to travel, to raise a family, to form private agreements, to enjoy privacy, or to live in peace. These are self-evident. They existed long before 1791 and they exist today.

The Ninth Amendment is proof that the founders themselves recognized this truth. They wrote it so no official could ever claim that silence in the Constitution means absence of rights. They admitted that rights are countless, that listing them all is impossible, and that the people retain every one.

The sovereign man or woman must remember this when rulers attempt deception. Officials often argue that if a right is not listed, it does not exist. They use this argument to deny freedom of movement, to impose regulations on family life, to demand licenses for natural acts, and to create obligations never agreed to. The Ninth Amendment destroys this argument. It says clearly that unlisted rights remain with the people.

Think of the maxim: silence does not equal surrender. The absence of a written line does not erase a birthright. The right exists because life exists, not because paper records it. The Ninth Amendment confirms that the absence of words does not mean the absence of sovereignty.

Consider practical examples. Nowhere does the Constitution mention the right to travel freely. Yet that right is obvious. Movement is part of life. To confine without cause is slavery. The Ninth Amendment affirms that such a right remains, even though not listed.

Nowhere does the Constitution mention the right to choose education for your children. Yet that right is natural. Parents are responsible for raising their offspring, not the state. The Ninth Amendment protects this by recognizing rights beyond writing.

Nowhere does the Constitution list the right to privacy in personal affairs. Yet the right exists. You are not required to share your life with rulers. The Ninth Amendment affirms that privacy is retained even without explicit mention.

The Constitution of one declares that the Ninth Amendment is a direct admission by rulers that they cannot limit freedom to what they wrote. It is evidence that sovereignty is broader than statutes. It is testimony that liberty extends into every corner of life, whether recorded or not.

This amendment is perhaps the strongest evidence for the sovereign perspective. It shows that rights come first, paper second. It shows that the people retain powers that no government can list away. It shows that the Constitution itself admits its incompleteness. The true constitution is the living man or woman.

The Ninth Amendment is the hidden jewel of the Bill of Rights because it removes every excuse rulers use to limit freedom. It denies the argument that rights exist only when written. It denies the claim that silence equals consent. It denies the presumption that the state defines the boundaries of liberty. Instead, it proclaims that liberty is vast, that rights are countless, and that all remain with the people.

Officials rarely mention the Ninth Amendment. Schools barely teach it. Courts treat it as decoration. Why? Because it is dangerous to the system. If people understood its meaning, most statutes would collapse.

Every claim of authority would be questioned. Every demand for licenses would be exposed as deception. The Ninth Amendment pulls back the curtain and reveals the truth: the list is not the limit.

The sovereign man or woman lives by this principle daily. When told that a right does not exist because it is not written, the sovereign answers with the Ninth Amendment. When asked for proof that freedom of travel, privacy, or association is recognized, the sovereign points to the amendment that says rights exist even when unlisted. This is the remedy against the deception of omission.

Think of the maxim: what is not forbidden is permitted. The state reverses this, claiming that what is not written is forbidden. The Ninth Amendment restores the correct order. It confirms that absence of words does not erase presence of rights.

Consider family life. Parents have the natural right to guide their children. Yet officials demand licenses for schooling, permits for activities, and approvals for medical choices. They act as though the state owns the child. The Ninth Amendment rejects this. It affirms that rights not written, such as parental authority, remain with the people.

Consider property. You have the natural right to use your land, build upon it, and cultivate it. Yet zoning laws and permits restrict these acts. Officials argue that no such right is listed, so it must be regulated. The Ninth Amendment exposes this as fraud. Rights to property use are retained even when not written.

Consider travel. Movement is part of existence. Yet governments demand licenses, registrations, and fees for the simple act of going from place to place. They argue that driving is a privilege, not a right. The Ninth Amendment proves otherwise. Travel existed before cars, before roads, before statutes. It remains a right, regardless of paperwork.

The amendment also protects the right to contract privately. Men and women have always exchanged goods and services without oversight. Statutes seek to regulate every transaction. Yet the Ninth Amendment confirms that the right to contract exists beyond writing. No paper can erase it.

The Constitution of one sees the Ninth Amendment as the broadest shield. It confirms that sovereignty cannot be confined to a list. It affirms that freedom extends wherever life extends. It declares that unspoken rights are still rights.

The amendment also proves that the framers feared central power. They knew rulers would argue that silence meant absence. They wrote the Ninth to prevent that lie. They admitted that they could not list everything. They confessed that freedom cannot be cataloged. This confession is now your evidence.

Living this truth requires courage. Officials will insist that unlisted rights are imaginary. They will mock claims of sovereignty. They will demand statutes as proof. The sovereign replies with the Ninth Amendment. It says plainly that rights exist beyond the text. It cannot be denied without denying the amendment itself.

The maxim of law holds: absence of evidence is not evidence of absence. The Ninth embodies this maxim. It affirms that the absence of a written right is not proof that the right does not exist. It is proof that rights are greater than paper.

The chapter closes with a reminder: the Ninth Amendment is your open door. It is your testimony that life itself is the source of freedom. It is the admission by rulers that they cannot confine liberty to ink. The list is not the limit. The Constitution of one is living proof that you carry every right within you, written or not.

Chapter 11: The Tenth Amendment – The Power of the People

The Tenth Amendment is the closing declaration of the Bill of Rights, and it speaks with clarity about where true power resides. It states: "The powers not delegated to the United States by the Constitution, nor prohibited by it to the States, are reserved to the States respectively, or to the people."

These words remind us that the federal government is not supreme. It is limited, delegated, and bound. Its powers exist only because the people allowed them. Anything not specifically granted remains with the people themselves or with their states. The amendment rejects the idea of unlimited authority. It affirms that sovereignty belongs at the bottom, not the top.

The Constitution of one interprets this amendment as a mirror of the sovereign individual. Just as government cannot take rights not granted, no man can take powers from another without consent. Authority flows upward, not downward. The individual is the root. Families and communities form from individuals. States form from communities. The federal government is last in line, created by compact, not by birthright.

Officials often ignore this. They act as though Washington holds supreme authority in every matter. They create agencies that regulate every corner of life. They expand powers never delegated. They claim jurisdiction far beyond what was written. This is dishonor.

The Tenth Amendment proves their deception. If the power was not delegated, it remains with the people.

Think about the word "delegated." To delegate is to grant temporarily. Delegated power is not surrendered. It is loaned. The people remain the true holders. They may withdraw delegation if it is abused. This principle is the essence of sovereignty. Delegated power is never permanent. It is conditional upon trust and honor.

The amendment also uses the word "reserved." This means set aside, kept back, not surrendered. All powers not given away remain with the people. This is a sweeping statement. It covers every area of life not specifically listed in the Constitution. Education, health, trade, land, family, and countless other matters remain with the people or their states. The federal government has no lawful authority in these areas unless consent is given.

The maxim of law holds that the greater includes the lesser. The sovereign individual holds the greatest power over his life. He may delegate some to community or state. But what is not given is retained. The federal government, being furthest removed, holds the least. The Tenth Amendment is written proof of this order.

Consider how this applies today. Federal agencies dictate schooling, health care, farming, energy, and even speech. None of these powers were delegated. They are usurpations. The amendment exposes them.

It declares that such powers were reserved. They remain with the people. The sovereign man or woman may point to this as evidence that overreach is unlawful.

The Constitution of one also recognizes that states reflect the sovereignty of individuals. Just as each person is a constitution of one, each state is a constitution of many. The federal government is a compact among states, not their master. The Tenth Amendment affirms this federal structure. It reminds rulers that Washington is servant, not king.

History shows why this amendment matters. The founders feared central power. They knew that distant authority tends to grow unchecked. They wrote the Tenth to restrain it. They wanted future generations to remember that the union was limited. They wanted the people to retain the final say. The amendment is their warning against empire.

The Tenth Amendment is a constant reminder that the people never surrendered their sovereignty. They delegated certain tasks to a federal authority, but delegation is not surrender. Delegation can be revoked. Power remains with the source. That source is the people themselves.

Officials dislike this truth because it strips them of their illusion of supremacy. They claim that federal law is always supreme, that agencies hold binding authority, that their jurisdiction extends everywhere. But the amendment contradicts them. Supremacy belongs only in the areas where power was delegated. Beyond that, authority is reserved. It is not theirs. It is ours.

The sovereign man or woman must understand that this principle applies on every level. The individual is sovereign first. Communities are sovereign second. States are sovereign third. The federal government is last. This order reflects natural law. It begins with the living and flows upward. Authority cannot lawfully flow downward unless consent is given.

Consider how often the Tenth Amendment is ignored. Federal agencies regulate agriculture even though farming is local. They regulate education even though schooling belongs to families and communities. They regulate health even though care is personal. These are usurpations. The amendment exposes them as dishonor. None of these powers were delegated. They remain reserved.

Think again about the word "reserved." Reserved means kept back, not surrendered, held in trust. This single word destroys the claim of unlimited federal power. If a power was not delegated, it is reserved. That is the end of the matter. No statute, agency, or decree can erase this truth.

The maxim of law says that delegated authority cannot exceed its source. If the people did not hold a power, they could not delegate it. For example, no individual has the natural right to enslave another. Therefore the people could not delegate a power of slavery to government. The same logic applies today. If no individual has the right to regulate the education of another's child, the people cannot delegate that power to Washington. The Tenth Amendment enshrines this principle.

The Constitution of one interprets this as both shield and sword. It is a shield against federal overreach. It is a sword to reclaim sovereignty. When officials claim jurisdiction where none was delegated, the Tenth Amendment is evidence against them. It proves that the power is reserved. It shifts the burden back to the accuser.

History provides examples of this principle in action. States have resisted federal mandates when they overstep. Communities have asserted their own authority against distant bureaucrats. Individuals have refused compliance when statutes reached beyond delegation. Each of these acts reflects the spirit of the Tenth Amendment.

The sovereign man or woman must also remember that the amendment mentions both states and the people. This balance matters. States are not masters. They are servants, just as the federal government is servant. The people remain the final authority. States may exercise powers not given to Washington, but those powers are still limited by the sovereignty of the individual. The amendment is not a license for state tyranny. It is recognition of distributed authority.

Living the Tenth Amendment means standing firm in your own sovereignty. It means remembering that no distant official has lawful power over your daily life unless you consent. It means recognizing that families, communities, and individuals retain all authority not delegated. It means refusing to surrender to usurpation disguised as law.

The chapter closes with this truth: the Tenth Amendment is the final wall in the Bill of Rights. It declares that the people remain the source of all power. It affirms that government is servant, not master. It testifies that what is not delegated is reserved. The Constitution of one lives this truth daily. The sovereign man or woman knows that power begins with the individual and ends only where consent allows it.

Chapter 12: The Constitution of One – Living Sovereignty

The Bill of Rights was written as evidence that freedom belongs to the people. Each amendment is a reminder that government is bound, not the sovereign. But the Constitution of one goes deeper. It declares that sovereignty is not limited to parchment or institutions. It is personal. It is lived. It begins and ends with the individual man or woman who chooses to stand in truth.

The phrase "Constitution of one" captures this reality. You are a living constitution. Your body is your jurisdiction. Your mind is your lawmaker. Your conscience is your judge. Your honor is your enforcement. You do not wait for officials to hand you freedom. You live it by recognizing it within yourself.

This does not mean isolation. Sovereignty is not withdrawal from the world. It is participation on your own terms. It is the power to enter agreements voluntarily and to walk away from contracts made in dishonor. It is the ability to speak freely, defend yourself, keep your home private, demand due process, and insist on judgment by peers. These are not theories. They are daily practices.

Living sovereignty begins with knowledge. Most people remain enslaved because they do not know they are free. They accept licenses as if they were rights. They accept taxes as if they were duties. They accept surveillance as if it were safety.

The Constitution of one begins when you see through the illusion. When you remember that rights come from life, not from government, you begin to reclaim them.

The next step is speech. Silence is taken as consent. That is why rulers encourage it. They prefer quiet submission. The sovereign speaks. He or she asks for proof. He or she demands contract. He or she refuses assumption. Each word spoken in honor collapses presumption. Living sovereignty means never allowing silence to be mistaken for agreement.

Defense is also essential. A sovereign who cannot defend is vulnerable to force. The Second Amendment affirms that defense is natural. To live sovereignty means to accept the responsibility of protection. This is not aggression. It is duty. You protect your life, your family, and your community.

You do not outsource this entirely to others. You stand ready as a free man or woman.

The home remains the heart of sovereignty. Living sovereignty means treating your home as your castle. You decide who enters. You decide how it is used. You refuse intrusions without consent. You do not surrender your threshold to policies or inspections. You guard it as the foundation of your independence.

Privacy is also vital. In a world of surveillance, living sovereignty means drawing firm boundaries. You choose what to share and what to withhold. You recognize that your papers, your property, your communications are yours by right.

You refuse to allow officials to treat you as transparent to their gaze. You live as though the Fourth Amendment were written on your heart, not just on parchment.

Living sovereignty also requires the discipline of honor. Freedom without honor becomes chaos. The sovereign does not harm others. He does not take without agreement. She does not deceive. They live by the maxim: do no harm, cause no loss, commit no fraud. These principles require no legislature. They are written in conscience. To live them is to prove sovereignty.

The Constitution of one also means responsibility for contracts. You speak for yourself. Your agreements bind you because you chose them. You do not blame others for your choices. You do not sign in ignorance. You do not surrender your word lightly. Sovereignty means your yes means yes and your no means no. This discipline builds trust. It strengthens community.

This chapter affirms that sovereignty is not a theory in books. It is a practice in life. Every day presents choices. Will you act as sovereign or as subject? Will you consent without thought, or will you demand proof? Will you live by conscience, or by fear? These choices define the Constitution of one.

Living sovereignty is not about claiming authority over others. It is about mastering yourself. The Constitution of one teaches that you are your own lawmaker. You cannot control others, nor should you seek to.

Your duty is to govern yourself with honor and to stand firm when others attempt to govern you without consent. This balance is the foundation of true freedom.

When you stand in sovereignty, officials will often test you. They will send notices demanding payment. They will attempt to search without warrant. They will issue summonses addressed to the legal fiction. These are tests. They rely on assumption. If you comply without question, the assumption hardens into obligation. If you ask for proof, the illusion collapses. Living sovereignty means choosing to respond with clarity, not fear.

The maxim of law says: he who does not deny, admits. This is why the sovereign always answers dishonor with rebuttal. You do not ignore. You do not run. You respond with honor. You say: I do not consent. Show me the contract. Prove the claim. Without proof, there is no obligation. Living sovereignty means placing the burden back where it belongs, on the one who makes the claim.

Another mark of sovereignty is calmness. The system thrives on conflict. It wants you to lash out in anger so it can brand you as rebellious. The sovereign refuses this trap. You remain calm, composed, and honorable. You stand in truth, not in rage. Living sovereignty means responding with dignity, even under pressure. Your strength is in your composure.

Responsibility is also central. The sovereign man or woman does not run from duty. If you harm another, you make it right.

If you cause loss, you restore it. If you commit fraud, you correct it. Sovereignty is not a license for recklessness. It is the discipline of accountability. Living sovereignty means owning your actions fully and correcting dishonor when it arises.

Community is strengthened when individuals live sovereignty. Families that teach honor raise children who respect freedom. Communities that respect property and privacy build trust. States that respect the Tenth Amendment protect their people from central control. The Constitution of one spreads outward, from individual to family to community to state, creating a living republic built on honor.

Living sovereignty also means rejecting fear. The system uses fear as its strongest weapon. Fear of punishment. Fear of ridicule. Fear of exclusion. Fear is the chain that keeps people silent and obedient. The sovereign man or woman cuts that chain by remembering that rights come from life itself. No statute can erase them. No official can take them. Fear loses its power when you remember who you are.

The Bill of Rights is evidence. It is valuable because it testifies to truths already known. But the deeper truth is the Constitution of one. You are free because you are alive. You are sovereign because you consent only to what is honorable. You are untouchable when you live in truth. This recognition is the greatest shield you can carry.

The chapter closes with this call: live your sovereignty daily. Speak when silence would be taken as consent. Defend when force threatens your life or property. Guard your home as your castle. Demand due process before yielding to any claim. Insist on trial by jury when accused. Reject cruel or excessive punishment. Claim rights beyond writing. Remember that power remains with the people.

The Constitution of one is not theory. It is life. It is the choice to live in truth, honor, and freedom. It is the recognition that you are the source of rights, not paper, not officials, not rulers. You are the sovereign. You are the constitution. You are the law of your own life.

Conclusion

The Bill of Rights was written as a covenant, but not between government and rulers. It was written between the people and their own posterity. It stands as a reminder that freedom is inherited, not granted. It is a record of principles that already existed and will always exist as long as men and women live in truth.

This covenant is living because it does not depend on parchment. Paper fades. Ink dries. Statutes are amended. Courts twist words. Yet the truth remains. Sovereignty is born with you. It cannot be given and it cannot be taken. It can only be forgotten. The Constitution of one is the memory that restores it.

The amendments we have studied each point to this reality. The First confirms your voice. The Second confirms your defense. The Third confirms your home. The Fourth confirms your privacy. The Fifth confirms your protection against compulsion. The Sixth and Seventh confirm the jury as shield. The Eighth confirms dignity against cruelty. The Ninth confirms that rights extend beyond writing. The Tenth confirms that power begins with the people. Together they form a circle of protection, a wall of testimony around the sovereign.

But the real covenant is not written in these ten amendments. It is written in conscience. It is written in the maxim that no man may harm another. It is written in the truth that consent is required for obligation.

It is written in the knowledge that every man's house is his castle, every woman's word is her bond, and every living soul is sovereign. This covenant cannot be repealed. It cannot be erased. It can only be ignored or remembered.

The system thrives on forgetfulness. Schools teach obedience instead of sovereignty. Media glorifies authority instead of freedom. Courts enforce statutes instead of honor. The result is a population that forgets its own covenant. Men and women accept licenses instead of rights, punishments instead of remedies, servitude instead of liberty. They live as tenants on their own land, as subjects in their own homes, as fictions in their own names.

The Constitution of one awakens memory. It reminds you that freedom is not a permission slip. It is not an indulgence granted by rulers. It is your birthright. To live it, you must stand in truth. You must reject contracts made without consent. You must refuse silence when silence is taken as agreement. You must guard your body, your property, your family, and your word. You must live honor daily.

This is the living covenant. It is not about rebellion. It is not about anger. It is about responsibility. It demands more of you than obedience ever could. A subject obeys and blames rulers for his fate. A sovereign lives in truth and accepts responsibility for his choices. That is the price of freedom. That is the covenant you inherit and pass on.

The founders knew this. That is why they wrote the Bill of Rights. They did not believe it created freedom. They believed it testified to what was already there. They hoped future generations would remember. The Ninth Amendment, in particular, is their confession that rights extend far beyond their list. They admitted that freedom cannot be confined to ten articles. They placed the burden on you to live sovereignty in every area of life.

The living covenant is not bound to history alone. It is present now. Every day, officials present claims against you. They send notices demanding payment. They enforce policies that assume your consent. They threaten punishment if you do not comply. Each of these moments is a test of sovereignty. Will you act as a subject, or will you stand as a sovereign?

To act as a subject is to comply without question. It is to sign without reading. It is to pay without demanding proof. It is to allow silence to be mistaken for agreement. This path is easy in the short term, but it leads to bondage. Each act of compliance strengthens the illusion that you are property of the state.

To act as a sovereign is harder. It requires awareness and courage. It requires you to ask questions others avoid. It requires you to demand contracts, to rebut assumptions, to insist on due process. It requires you to speak in honor when silence would be safer. But this path leads to freedom. Each act of sovereignty weakens the illusion. Each demand for proof exposes the fraud. Each rebuttal restores the covenant.

The covenant also requires community. Sovereignty is personal, but it is not selfish. A free man or woman respects the sovereignty of others. You do not harm, steal, or deceive. You respect property, contracts, and privacy. You speak truth, even when unpopular. By living in honor, you strengthen the covenant for everyone. Communities built on sovereign individuals are strong, resilient, and free.

The Bill of Rights is the record of this covenant, but the Constitution of one is its living form. You are the evidence that freedom exists. You are the proof that sovereignty cannot be erased. You are the covenant made flesh. The system wants you to forget this. It wants you to believe that freedom is fragile, dependent on elections, statutes, and courts. The truth is that freedom is as strong as your will to live it.

This book has walked through each amendment as testimony. But the testimony is not the end. The end is you. The Constitution of one is not written in Washington. It is written in your conscience. It is not argued by politicians. It is lived by men and women who refuse to surrender. It is not secured by armies. It is secured by honor, truth, and responsibility.

The living covenant is a promise. It is the promise that you will not forget who you are. It is the promise that you will not trade sovereignty for convenience. It is the promise that you will stand in honor even when tested. It is the promise that you will pass this truth to your children and to your community.

If you live this promise, no ruler can enslave you. They may threaten, but they cannot bind without consent. They may punish, but they cannot erase dignity. They may regulate, but they cannot touch the source of rights. That source is you.

The final call is simple. Remember. Speak. Defend. Guard. Respect. Stand. Live as the Constitution of one. You are the covenant. You are the sovereign. You are free.

About the Author

Roger Davies researches the crossroads of commerce, policy, and personal sovereignty. He writes for readers who sense there is more to the story, who are ready to replace fear with honour and paperwork with plain truth.

When not writing, he helps men and women organise their records, challenge unfounded claims, and build communities grounded in mutual aid and responsibility.

www.ingramcontent.com/pod-product-compliance
Lightning Source LLC
LaVergne TN
LVHW022025200926
848481LV00007B/2541
* 9 7 9 8 2 3 2 9 1 2 3 3 8 *